Antonio T. Smith Jr. Changed Our Lives

Stories To Inspire You To Plant Better

Dr Patrick Businge

Greatness University Publishers
info@greatness-university.com
www.greatness-university.com

ISBN: 978-1-9999494-1-9
ISBN-13: 978-1-9999494-1-9

DEDICATION

This book is dedicated to three people groups. My fans, the 25 authors who honored me by penning this book and my team. I am most grateful. I can think of the many bad things I have been called in my life. I must admit, I have deserved them all. I have not always been who I am today. You will read great things about me but I have not always been great. These authors will spill their hearts on paper. There have been times I have spilled hearts in real life. To say that I have changed lives is a concept I still cannot wrap my head around. After all, I'm just a kid from the hood.

Nobody ever gave me anything. Some would say I was born in the wrong family and some would say I should be a statistic. Through it all, I have the opportunity to witness my funeral while I'm still living. That's how I view this book. This book is my funeral. Every day I wake in the morning, I ask myself these three questions:

- What do I feel is impossible in my field, but if it could be done would fundamentally change my business?

- What breaks my heart?

- What do I want people to line up and thank me for at the end of my life?

I'd like to think these three questions were the genesis of my actions which eventually spawn this book. I am truly grateful.

I am so in love with life and I am so in love with you. My number one core belief is that we are all connected. What I am, you are. What you are, I am. Essentially, there is only one of us in the room. Therefore, whatever these authors have said about me, they've also said about themselves. I'm ever so thankful to all my fans. The thought of even having fans, to me, is out of this world. I didn't dribble my way to fame. I didn't catch or kick a ball to it either, nor did I get a wooden stick and it one. I served my way to fame. The path I have led was never glorious. I put others before me. I made a lot of people a lot of money and I made a lot of smiles happy to smile. Moreover, I am grateful for every last one of you fans.

I now understand how rock stars feel when they say, "Without you, there would be no me!" Not only is this book my funeral that I get to see whole I am living, this book is also an Oscar for the movie of my life. Oh, I am ever so grateful. I am surrounded by the greatest team to ever be assembled. Although I receive a lot of credit. Some of which I deserve. Some of which I do not. My team is the reason I wake up in the morning. Team. This is such a broad word for people I love so much. In some cases, my team is family. In most cases, my team are people I've met within the last seven years. Please know, none of us were great, at least by worldly standards. We were ordinary people making extraordinary decisions.

Antonio T. Smith Jr. Changed Our Lives

If you ask me if I deserve this book, my answer would be "No", but my heart would secretly say yes. No, because I have learned behaviors that allow me to remain humble, focused and to give credit to others. Yet, I do deserve this book. This is not an arrogant statement, but an awareness-statement. There is a law of this universe that gives you a harvest every single time you plant a seed. Ladies and gentlemen, I have planted trillions of seeds into millions of people. By law, this book, the 25 authors, of whom more than a few are celebrities is simply a result of all those seeds planted. I wish you a good life. I wish nothing but prosperity for you. I wish for everyone who is to read this book to not only be inspired by these words but to set your life on a path in which something similar will happen to you. May your days be splendid and your motives change your life. If you learn nothing from this book, please learn this one concept. We're all connected and I love you like I love myself.

Lastly, thank you so much to one of the greatest mentors on earth, Mr. Les Brown. Likewise, thank you to one of the greatest friends that I have, Serena Brown Travis. There is no doubt that my life has changed for the better for meeting you both. I do not deserve either one of you. It could be said that no one does. There was no benefit whatsoever for either of you to co-sign this book. You did it for me. You did it for me because that's just the kind of people you are. Les, you allowed me to share the stage with you and Serena, you allowed me to share life with you. There is no way I could ever repay you both but I will do my very best to return the favor. You can plant better, you can dominate!

Antonio T. Smith, Jr.

CONTENTS

CONTENTS BY CO-AUTHOR

ACKNOWLEDGMENTS

This book is the result of the hard work of celebrity researcher Dr. Patrick Businge of the United Kingdom. It is also a result of the hard work of the 25 authors who gave a bit of themselves so I can be whole. Although it rarely gets said, this book is also a result of the silent-hard-work of Elishia Smith who allows me to travel the world as she takes care of our children. I would do an absolute disservice if I did not recognize this magnificent sacrifice.

To my team, Tempestt S. Smith, Deaunna Mitchell, Grace Sandles, Shannon Clark, Rev. Bryant Johnson and Michelle Mueller, I could do none of this without you. You have sat with me many hours helping me make all our dreams come true. Thank you. I love you. Let it be acknowledged that the Greatness University Publishers published this book and took on all the financial responsibilities to make this possible. They have coordinated every effort and I am grateful.

I would like to acknowledge Pastor Joel Osteen of Lakewood Church for being the greatest leader I have ever known. In 2012, Pastor Joel took me under his wings for two years and taught me how to be the leader I am today. I could never acknowledge him enough for this. To Mr. Les Brown, one of the greatest speakers to ever live, thank you for taking a rising star and giving me a platform that made me a

Supernova. Thank you to Serena Brown Travis for teaching me how to do mega business as a mega speaker.

Lastly, I acknowledge myself for working hard to develop the character that did not allow all of this to blow up in my face. I want to thank everyone who ever said anything positive to me and to anyone who ever taught me anything. I promise I applied it all. To all the haters and antagonist that I attracted into my life from either having a low level of awareness or just being great. I appreciate the experiences but I'm not naming none of you. I leave you with this quote from a regular carpenter that irregularly inspired the world: "By this my Father is glorified, that you bear much fruit and so prove to be my disciples."

Foreword

Les Brown
World's Greatest Motivational
Speaker

Foreword

I often say, "You have something special. You have greatness within you!" When I met Antonio T. Smith, Jr. I knew I met someone with an extraordinary gift. What amazed me is Antonio's drive. Based on his circumstances, his violent beginnings, and unsettled childhood, Antonio had every reason to remain *Stuck*, but somehow, in spite of his circumstances, Antonio is a man on a mission, who is *Hungry* for success.

As a business advisor to Les Brown Unlimited, his work and impact is clear. His business acumen and integrity are unparalleled. I could go on and on about his achievements. I am a proud mentor and grateful that our paths have crossed.

As you read this book, look at the common themes, his strategies for greatness, and his unwavering faith. We can all learn so much from this young man's life.

I present to you, Antonio T. Smith, Jr. Changed Our Lives.

Les Brown
World's Greatest Motivational Speaker

Foreword

Serena Brown Travis
The Pulpit Chic

Foreword

Antonio T. Smith, Jr. is a stellar example of business excellence, master of motivation, and a man making major moves. Since knowing Antonio, my business has expanded as he has an eagles eye for wealth, financial advancement, and complete domination.

On a personal note, I can attest that Antonio T. Smith, Jr. has changed my life. His story alone is both chilling and incredible. Once speaking with him about his time living homeless, hungry, and abused as a child, I asked myself, "How can he be so optimistic, encouraging, as a pillar of hope and agent of change?" And the answer is clear, God has blessed everything and everyone Antonio encounters." No wonder there is a complete book honoring and highlighting his success.

As the daughter of the great Les Brown, one would assume my confidence and high self-esteem remains at an all-time high, but just like anyone else, I need reminders, a helping hand, and a listening ear. Antonio is my mentor with valuable insights. He is my prayer partner who seems to have a special connection with God, along with a genuine and humble spirit, never forgetting his humble beginnings.

Looking back over the course of our relationship, I can honestly recall the moments where I gave up and then I'd receive a call from Antonio, reminding me of my title, role, and anointing over my life. His words of affirmation stirred up my gift and I am more than honored to say, Antonio T. Smith, Jr. CHANGED MY LIFE!

Serena Brown Travis
The Pulpit Chic

Introduction

Mentor, Coach, Millionaire Maker, Bestselling Author

Who is Antonio T. Smith Jr?

Antonio T. Smith, Jr. is a prolific public speaker certified by Les Brown, the world's greatest motivational speaker, who has delivered over 2000 keynotes at events such as the University of Houston, Wiley College, which you can listen to on his podcast. Antonio is an internationally recognized trainer and speaker, and best-selling author in self-help and religious categories. He specializes in Cognitive Behavior Therapy, Business and Strength Training, Leadership, Teleconference Presentations, Personal Breakthroughs, Prosperity Consciousness, Mindset Training, and all levels of effective marketing, as well as scholarship in the Old Testament and Jewish Covenants. Antonio also owns one of the most successful technology companies in Texas. He holds a bachelor's in Christianity and a Master's in Theological Studies.

Antonio T. Smith, Jr. is a best-selling author and a popular podcast host with a show that reaches over 70 countries and 60 different languages. He has been coaching people around the world on personal transformation for the last 9 years and reaches over hundreds of thousands of listeners across the globe.

Antonio overcame abandonment, homelessness, and brokenness. He had to learn at the tender age of six how to use his mind to climb out of sleeping in a dumpster. He would spend his entire childhood homeless, was adopted when he was 14, and aged out of CPS custody at 18 years old. This Galveston, TX native has been through more in his 30+ years than most will ever experience. He has developed a "plant better" attitude, in which he teaches people to plant better seeds in order to have a better life. Antonio has developed coaching tools, programs, courses and books designed to help the world succeed. Today he is a certified Les Brown Partner, a world renown public speaker, and leadership coach.

Antonio Smith Jr. graduated from the Houston Baptist University twice. First, with his bachelors of arts in Christianity, as the president of the Theta Kappa Alpha Religious Studies and Theology Honor Society. Second, with his Masters of Arts in Theological Studies, while graduating with the highest GPA in his class. Smith, has served as pastor of a small Baptist church in Galveston, Texas for over five years, and in one of the most sought after preachers in South East Texas. He travels the world giving theological lectures and has taught classes such as Eschatology, Old Testament, New Testament, Paul and His Letters, and Old Testament Covenants, in a few colleges and universities in the Greater Houston Area. Based on his rich academic and business experience, he founded ATS Business University that I am happy to introduce you to on the next pages.

ATS Business University

ATS Business University

ATS Business University launched 2018 but has been in the works for years. Antonio T. Smith Jr. has always had a passion for teaching people everything he knows and helping them avoid mistakes that he and others have made. With so many new businesses opening at a rapid pace, and with a strong desire to help these businesses become the best that they can be, starting an exclusive business training program was a no brainer.

This interactive training program focuses on business training, marketing training, personal development training, and sales training. Research indicate that over 95% of all new businesses fail within the first 5 years because of lack of profits. The ATS Business University is the solution to that problem. In all things, ATS Jr. Companies makes profitable clients more profitable and the ATS Business University is an extension of this promise. Unlike most training programs, incoming entrepreneurs must be willing to put in work. It is more than watching videos, taking notes and attending events.

The ATS Business University holds people accountable for their actions or lack thereof. As the ATS Jr. Companies believes, "harvest doesn't lie." Meaning you can pretend but your business will always tell on you regarding how much time, energy and effort you put into it. Each member is welcomed and put through an on-boarding process that introduces them to the program, sets expectations, walks members through the technology that is used, gets to know each person's goals and desires and sets the tone for the type of hands-on experience they will receive. From there, each member is then assigned an ambassador, who not only reminds them of live trainings, but conducts 3 mentor calls that includes homework, progress reports and forward movements. The ATS Business University does not allow people to walk to profitable status alone.

With 4 membership levels to choose from, incoming members not only receives lifetime memberships, but they receive multiple weekly live trainings, that focuses on sales, marketing, and business. What makes this program different is the intentional emphasis that is put on personal development. Live trainings also includes: Plant Better Sundays led by Antonio T. Smith Jr., Let's Talk Tuesday, and Walk It Out Wednesday's. Plant Better Sundays is a live training that occurs every Sunday evening, focuses on motivating individuals to prepare to dominate for the upcoming week. Let's Talk Tuesdays, occurs every Tuesday evening, features a member of the ATS Jr. Companies staff who includes, Bryant A. Johnson, Deaunna M. Mitchell, Grace Y. Sandles, Michelle L. Mueller, Shannon R. Clark and Tempestt S. Smith. Each week a member of the team coaches and leads discussions based on the topic of the week.

Antonio T. Smith Jr. Changed Our Lives

Let's Talk Tuesdays aims to help individuals reach the highest expression of themselves. Lastly, Walk It Out Wednesday's, led by Bryant A. Johnson, the Director of Spirituality at the ATS Jr. Companies, focuses on developing a vibrant and well thriving spirituality practice.

Members also receive access to playbacks of all training sessions, other online coaching courses such as Overcoming Low Self-Esteem led by Antonio T. Smith Jr. and Retraining Your Subconscious Mind led by Shannon R. Clark. Last but not least, ATS Business University members receive free access to ATS Jr. Companies other online training platform called Plant Better University. Plant Better University is a better-eLearning platform, that is constantly updated by and led by Antonio Smith. When you enroll to PBU, you get access to Antonio T. Smith, Jr., along with all of his proven tools, strategies, and resources, as well as his leading Strategic Coaches who have mastered his programs. Here, you will find how to unlock the highest expression of yourself.

This carefully designed platform includes tons of training on every entry level. Antonio is passionate about over delivering; therefore, you will discover when you enroll on a level, you are constantly upgraded and given more access to your current level. Members will have access to live training, seminars, on-demand videos, mindset phone calls, live events, and many other resources. Anyone can subscribe at any time and can work through the material at his or her own pace. The ATS Jr. Companies offers Plant Better University for those outside of the ATS Business University for $8.99/month. Plant Better University is coined as the "Netflix of personal development."

Angel
Talisha Thomas

Business Owner
www.bbetiquette1.wixsite.com/bbetiquette

Angel

Do you ever feel that no one can ever understand you or your problems? How about feeling hopeless? I felt that way at one point until I met Antonio Smith.

When I hear the name Antonio T. Smith and his team I think of an angel sent from heaven by God to guide me on this wonderful journey called "manifesting my life purpose." Antonio is a man of his word. His model "making profitable clients more profitable" isn't just words but truth. Antonio and his partner Tempestt have not only help me with my business but, also with my mindset. When times get tough I can always hear Antonio's voice in my head saying "keep moving forward." The ATS Jr. University (is how I got connected with such great people) don't treat you like a student or a client but, more like family. This university has become my home.

Antonio is the true definition of adding value. He doesn't just point out your flaws but, help you climb mountains so you can go through the healing process and learn from your pass. He has helped me expand the amount of money I desire. He has also helped me expand my limited beliefs and come up with a strategic plan. I belief Antonio would agree with me on this… He has the best team on earth to help build his legacy. They all are so passionate and eager to help. There is a no judgment zone in this family. He loves to share his books and knowledge in business and life that helped him become successful.

Although I haven't manifested anything yet it's coming! I read somewhere that anything great takes time. I have experienced personal growth and positive change in my life since being in the ATS University. The hardest thing for me was overcoming childhood trauma and a negative mindset. Antonio has a remedy for this: it is called "Planet Better Mindset". This was a process but as time passed by it gets a lot easier and the pain and hurt starts to evaporate as though it never existed. I am discovering that I am worthy of all my desires and that I already have them. There was a point where I didn't know how to handle my emotions. Of course you know who help me with that! I am growing and maturing because of the help from Antonio and his team. My spiritual growth has changed and I meditate daily. I am not the one to open up to strangers, but with his team I was comfortably able to tell my story. The bottom line is that you can't get this type of compassionate intellect from anywhere else.

So, who is this person that Antonio has opened his heart to? Well, my name is Talisha Thomas owner of Building Business Etiquette: a consultant firm located in Houston, TX. My consulting firm provides presence training and etiquette courses that help in the following areas: college readiness, career readiness, workforce development, and professional development. These areas are targeted to teens, young adults, business owners, managers, executives, and politicians to help develop their professional and social lives. Making it easier for them to become an outstanding leader, a potential hire and be able to perfect their purpose in life.

Believed

Deaunna Mitchell

25

Believed

Antonio always showed a belief in me that I never had in myself. This is where my life's story and my journey shifted. Have you ever come across anyone who pushed you for your dreams more than you pushed yourself? This is Antonio for me. It all started with his belief in me.

I met Antonio during my Sophomore year in high school at Ball High School in Galveston, TX. He was best friends with my grade school crush and we shared a couple of electives together. The first day I met him, he hit me with an energy that stayed with me for 20 years. Yes, 20 years. I did not know what it was then, I just knew that there was something about him. I ignored it then, of course. Why, because I was a teenager shaped and formed by what I was told to do and who I was told to be and not by what burned in me.

I am also a firm believer that everything happens for a reason. There is a reason why, at that time in my life, I rejected anything Antonio. Even then, he was an encourager. I watched him encourage his friends and our classmates and I never saw him with a frown on his face. All of this not knowing his story.

Like all associates and friends in high school, we parted ways only to come back together a few years later when he owned his record label. What do you know!!! I was a female artist on his label. I loved to sing. Always had and yet again, he believed in me and encouraged me and provided a way for me to be able to grow my passion. He nurtured my voice and even brought others in to help me write music and train me vocally. His belief in me was indescribable. By this time, I was in my early twenties, damaged and my mindset was that I was not good enough for anything. I wasn't anything and I would never be anything because, number one, I wasn't what my mother expected me to be and, number two, I wasn't what I believed my family was proud of. I believed that I was unwanted and unloved. I allowed this to pull me away from the one person who believed enough in me to take a chance on me: Antonio. So, I parted ways at this time.

He never left me, Antonio. I mean, he was always in my thoughts. I have had a lot of people tell me that they believed in me, but no one took the time to help me and nurture whatever they saw in me. It hurts when you want something so badly but have no clue of where to start. Everyone keeps telling you that you have so much potential but won't take two steps forward to instruct you or even give you the tools. If they do instruct you, they do it in a way that is more so using you as a tool to for them and not allowing you to grow within your strengths. That's where Antonio was different. He took the steps with me and gave me the tolls that I needed to change my path.

Antonio and I crossed paths again in 2010. He had

started a new business venture and he wanted me to be a part of it because it worked so amazingly for him. Me remembering who he was and seeing that he had not changed, I took a chance because he always took a chance on me. I met him at a steak house on 45 North in Houston, TX. What I was shown was something that I knew would work for me because Antonio had his hands in it.

By this time, I was completely submerged in my low self-esteem and self-worth and anything "self" related. I had gained so much weight that I barely looked at myself in the mirror when I got dressed, if I got dressed. I was living with my father and attempting to do something that I really didn't want to do but convinced myself to because I was a people pleaser and wanted the approval of my mother. So, hearing from Antonio, the one person who always believed in me and took chances on me, uplifted me.

The thing is, I couldn't enjoy that happiness because in my low self-esteem, low self-image and high self-doubt, I also believed that I was the poison in everyone's life. I therefore disconnected myself from Antonio because I didn't want to disappoint him like I have disappointed everyone else in my life. So yet again, I said good bye to the light that was cast upon the road that I was supposed to be on and went for the paved, well-lit road that I was still traveling on.

Antonio and I did not cross paths again until October 2015. We were Facebook friends and I watched his growth and change over the years. By this time, I had been married 5 years, working a job that I honestly didn't want, and my son was seven months old. I was 32. Life was not exactly what I had hoped it would be. It really came to a head after my son's birth. I did not suffer with post-partum, but I suffered with being dead while living. Since my son's birth, I had been crying myself to sleep and waking up with knots in my stomach. I felt completely alone, and I just knew that there was more for me.

So, I reached out to Antonio. I wanted to start my business up again. This time, I wasn't letting go and I was going to follow the light. However, it still took me until January 20, 2016 to make the decision to stay in the light this time and boy am I glad that I did. From this point on, Antonio nurtured me and gave me instructions on what to do with this burning desire that I had so deeply within me. He did something for me that no one else has ever done for me. He allowed and encouraged me to be me.

After 20+ years of not being me, I had absolutely no clue who "ME" was. That is when Antonio got to working and building and instructing. His Five Phases of Growth really did a number on me. How, because it was through his Five Phases of Growth that I was able to break down walls that I had built within myself and it was through these Five Phases that I was able to stop lying to myself about who I was and what I was.

There was a course that he taught, and I still can't get through the first video to this day, that completely change my life. "Overcoming Low-Self Esteem". There are a lot of people that have watched that and have complemented me on my transparency and growth, but only Antonio knew how hard recording that course was for me. Everything in that course hit home. He always knew what was needed and when it was needed to get you to grow up and that was what I needed to grow up. I am ashamed to admit that I have not sat through the class again because I am nervous about what walls will come down at that point. That is how powerful that course was and is.

Antonio took the time to show me where I was strong and help me to build in those strengths instead of keeping me in the shadows of my weaknesses. He also taught me to be transparent with myself and stop lying to myself and he guided me to be a better person. The biggest thing that Antonio taught me, the one thing that he did that saved my life and changed my world, was he show me "ME". He showed me the person everyone else saw. He showed me that it wasn't everyone else who was wrong but that I was the catalyst and that everything was my fault. When I allowed myself to accept this, this changed me as a person, as a friend, as a business woman, and as a mother. That was my biggest thing. The type of mother that I was to my son. Antonio showed me that I was making the same mistakes others had made and that I was creating another generation of brokenness with my son.

You want to know how Antonio changed my life? He allowed me to be me and guided me to be a better person. All this started with his belief in me when I did not believe in myself. His unwavering character and integrity kept me in check. It showed me who I was and his amazing ability to break down everything to my understanding. Antonio's teachings and continuous support has allowed me to grow in ways that I never imagined. I am now a millionaire because of Antonio!! Thank You Antonio!!!

Branded

Catherine Bennett

Founder of Massive Praise Ministries

Branded

Catherine Bennett is the founder of Massive Praise Ministries. It was founded on June 28, 2013 with the aim of giving young men and women who loved to dance for the Lord the opportunity to learn how to worship God from the inside out. This ministry has been used to educate them on how to be successful men and women. It provides food, blankets, gloves, socks Thanksgiving baskets, Easter baskets, and Christmas baskets to the less fortunate. Its ministers travel to different states in America changing the lives of young people, ministering to God's Kingdom and making a difference in the community.

I remember when I first met Antonio Smith, he was just a young boy coming to the Boys and Girls Club. Antonio would have conversations with my son any time they crossed paths. At his time, he was really a loner searching for his identity. In the process, he took some wrong turns. I never in a million year would have thought that this young boy would grow up to be a very successful entrepreneur and motivational speaker.

My journey with Atonio began in 2012-2014 when we were starting our dance ministry business called Massive Praise Ministries "The Next Level". Antonio guided us through the process every step of the way. We learned how to sell our brand and not the ministry. We came up with "Dance is Life" and he began to promote us as much as he could with flyers and slogans on Facebook every week. The brand began to take off and everyone was using it. Antonio later came to one of our rehearsal and did an informercial for us which is still making way through Facebook and Google. We began to learn how to become prosperous in our works because Antonio taught us how to only be affiliated with people who benefitted us that were in the same area of business.

Antonio was always a strong encouragement to our ministry. Every time we met, he always had goals for us to meet. Once we began to meet the high expectations that he had set for us, we began to take flight and the ministry is very successful at this present time. We have traveled to many states in America, ministered for National conferences, and opened for many artists for them to do their concerts.

Business
Jerome Redd

Speaker, Author, Actor, Comedian and
Entrepreneur
www.jeromeredd.com

Business

Jerome Redd is a dynamic, master motivational speaker, author, actor and standup comedian. He grew up on the improvised streets of Baltimore, Maryland. After graduating from High School, he spent 21 years working and later retired from the United States Army.

Jerome Redd has spoken before businesses, classrooms and school assemblies. While stationed overseas, he worked with youth groups and taught Sunday School to the local High School students. He is presently the head instructor for a local engineering firm (CONNOR) and speaks all over the United States to several companies, for this client.

He has published three books of poetry. Two of those books are specifically for youth and students. He has just finished a 3-book series about his seven years of service in Upstate State New York, working with students and young people locked up and his successful turn-around rate with them. His book is Titled: "Fixing The Broken, Without Being Broken." Here is his story on how Antonio Smith changed his life.

<u>Tell Me, Who Did I Just Give My Money Too?</u>

My name is Jerome Redd. I retired from the United States Army in 1996, after twenty-one years of faithful service. I spent seven years working at a boot-camp in upstate New York with delinquent youth, out of New York City. When I returned those young people to New York City, after six-months with me, I started receiving phone calls that I had actually reached some of those kids. I later left New York and returned to Baltimore, Maryland, my hometown.

The influence of my contact with those young people in New York continued once I arrived back home. They encouraged me to take my talent of writing very good poetry and to have it published. Notwithstanding, after the publishing of my third book, it confirmed that these young people knew exactly what they were talking about. Excited about this accomplishment, coupled with my success with those in New York, I felt compelled to write a novel about this experience. It is this compelling desire that ultimately placed me on a direct collision course with Mr. Antonio T. Smith Jr.

The composing and drafting of this book, started off very smooth. My excitement, my flow, my delivery, all confirmed a positive and large need to get this book written and to get it into the hands of the people. Unfortunately, I also ran into another obstacle. I was not completely satisfied with the method of how the book came together or how I had concluded it. I stopped writing and set the book aside for about six months. My determined resolution to complete this complicated problem balled down to going from one book to three books. That's right. A 3-book series was born from this dilemma.

At this point in time, I quickly realized that most authors don't come out of the gate with their first novel in a 3-book series. I concluded that this unique opportunity to write in this fashion required and needed an additional touch. This book needed the right person to write the Foreword. And let me make this perfectly clear to all of those who choose to read my 3-book series (**Fixing The Broken, Without Being Broken)**, Antonio T. Smith Jr., was not my first selection for the Foreword. Sadly, he was not my first choice. But, he was the right choice.

My first choice to write the Foreword was Les Brown. That's right, the same world renowned motivational speaker, was my first choice and I was determined to get him to do it. What I was unaware of at the time of my pursuit was that Antonio T. Smith Jr. was affiliated and well known by Les Brown. I reached out to the Les Brown organization about what it was going to take for me to organize a meeting with Mr. Brown. I was told that the best way to make this happen was to attend an upcoming Les Brown event. Since the writing of this book was going to include motivational speaking on my part anyway, attending a Les Brown event was a no-brainer. So, I paid my money and signed up. I was also told to bring a copy of my manuscript with me, which I did. In addition, I had no idea that Antonio T Smith Jr. was going to be there or part of the breakout session that Les Brown had included with his powerful program.

Upon arrival to this function in April 2018, I met Les Brown; shook hands with Les Brown; took a picture with Les Brown; gave a copy of my book to Les Brown; and I was told that we would talk about the Foreword later. Not to bad-mouth Mr. Brown or his people, I did not get to speak to him or anyone on his team for the next four-days about the issue of getting the Foreword of my book addressed. Notwithstanding, I still got a lot of valuable information and motivational speaking nuggets during this event from Les Brown and his team.

On the third day of this event, during a breakout session is when I was first introduced to Mr. Antonio T. Smith Jr. His presentation was the second session of three, which I got to attend. I arrived at his meeting about fifteen minutes after he had started his presentation. As I listened to the other thirty minutes of this his presentation, I was totally blown away and impressed with what he had to say. Yet, I was still missing the first fifteen minutes. As he concluded his talk, he offered everyone a special price, because we were in Les Brown's group. As much as I wanted to hear that first fifteen minutes, before I made a purchase, my instincts told me that a 90% discount, with this guy, was a no-brainer. So, I pulled out my credit card and I signed up. And as I was processing the credit card with one of his associates, I made it very clear that I'm not really sure exactly what I am signing up for. This explains why I had given this chapter the title: Tell Me, Who Did I Just Give My Money Too? I trust my instincts and my instincts made it clear to me that I would not regret this financial decision and that I can take this to the bank. I found out later that not only could I take it to the bank, but that I could even get interest on my investment.

After signing up with the ATS University on the third day of this event, the next day, I was also approached about an opportunity to be mentored under Les Brown as a motivational speaker. I then looked at this entire situation as either a win-win or it could it be a win-win-win. I am now part of the ATS University, I decided to join and be mentored by Les Brown, and I might be able to later get Les Brown to also do the Foreword for my book after all.

I initially came to this function to get Les Brown to do the Foreword to my upcoming 3-book series period. It is now my last day and we haven't spoken about my book or the Foreword at all. Notwithstanding, some positive things have really occurred regardless. Then something interesting happened. The night before I left this function, my roommate and I got into a conversation about Antonio and we began to compare notes. He even called Antonio from the room. I asked myself, Antonio is a millionaire and he just met him, how does he have Antonio's number? I was impressed. The next day my roommate and I were both headed to the airport together. While we were waiting for our lift to the airport, Antonio approached me. We exchanged salutations. I then told him that I hear some nice thing about him. He said that he had heard some nice things about me. I was at first taken back a little, because I came here alone and only a few people had gotten to know anything about me at all. But, Antonio didn't stop there. What he said next took my breathe away and left me speechless. He said, "How can I help you?" I said excuse me and he repeated himself. Unable to respond or comment, I could only think of my book and the Foreword. I asked him could he speak to Les Brown about doing my Foreword. He assured me that he speaks to Les Brown, a minimum of once a week and he will bring this issue up on my behalf.

As I gave Antonio a copy of my manuscript, I asked him if I could I get his phone number from my roommate. Antonio said sure and got into a car and drove away. While still in shock over what just happened, I needed a moment to get myself together. All of my life, I have asked others how could I be of service to them, but no one in the business world had ever asked that question of me. At that moment, Mr. Antonio T. Smith Jr., had gotten my attention and boy had he gotten my attention.

When I arrived back in Baltimore, it took me a couple of day to get myself together and get back into the swing of things. During that first week, I got a call from my Ambassador, Grace. She explains that her role is help, facilitate, assist and be my liaison with ATS University. Now the question is, was I expecting and Ambassador? The answer is no. How much does the Ambassador cost, I asked Grace? The answer is nothing. The Ambassador comes with your package. Grace, screened me and ask me questions about me and my business and my aspirations for the future. I was then blow away again. I am now repeating my previous questions of what have I really gotten myself into? The alarms bells were going off, but they were the good alarm bells. What in the world is going on? This hasn't happened to me before or I would have known it.

Next comes my first meeting/teaching over skype/zoom with Antonio. I'm very excited and have no clue as to what to expect or what was going to happen. I had a book, an ink pen and I was ready to take notes. Unfortunately, I didn't take a lot of notes. Antonio kind of started with me and made me the example for everyone to learn from. He first talked about selling people stuff that they don't need and that they don't want. He said, "Stop it." He then showed us how to poll your audience to find out what they really want and then create a product or value that they need. Then, sell it to them. He also mentioned using Google Trends to determine where you customers can be located and how to spend pennies on the dollar in advertising to sell your produce/services.

After he did this awesome job of explaining everything, he needed to use or give us an example. I became his example; his living example. I became his guinea pig. He asked me to unmute my microphone and he began to asked me about my 3-book series that I'm almost finished with. He then went on his computer, for all us viewers, typed in "3-Book Series" into Google Trends. Up pops, five foreign countries where 80% or more of readers purchase 3-book series. He then said if you advertise through Facebook to those five countries alone, your sale will be through the roof. Guess what Antonio did for a second time? He left me speechless. He didn't even touch Amazon, local book store, vending or book signing. He didn't even touch the US at all.

I quickly realized after that first session, that if I did what Antonio told me to do, I will not only get back every penny I spent to join his university, but I also get every penny back that I spent on my Les Brown package as well. Talk about a ROI (Return On Investment). I was blown away. The next two session were just like the first. He was always giving me value. Then I noticed that there were morning sessions and evening sessions. I also noticed that there weren't the same sessions and you could go back and download any sessions that you couldn't make. If you couldn't get on the computer, you could listen on your phone or in your car. Nobody in the industry is doing it the ATS way. The others can't touch Antonio T. Smith Jr. and ATS University.

I came to quickly realize that the ATS University financial decision, was a very smart decision. But I still didn't have the Foreword for my book done. In addition, in over the same thirty-day period of time with ATS University, I had only heard from the Les Brown's team once. Yet in contradiction, I'm in conversation with Antonio and Grace 3-5 time per week in some type of interaction that is giving me value and potential revenue. I then told Grace to tell Antonio the following. "I've got about 7-8 books that I am going to write, we'll let Les do one of those books, but I now want Antonio T. Smith Jr. to do this present book, not Les Brown." When I finally got to share this publicly with Antonio, he accepted my invitation, but he didn't stop there. He agreed to do the Foreword and stated before witnesses that he wouldn't charge me a dime. Within 2-3 weeks of my request, I received the Foreword. Guess what? I'm still working on the book.

Another astonishing thing about Antonio T. Smith Jr. is how he treats his customer; how he treats his employees; and how he treats his business associates. One of the attributes that I truly admire about

Antonio is the fact he does add value and he will expose your weakness. When those weaknesses are exposed, he tries to help people to see their own weakness and then assist them with options and alternatives to choose from so they can make their own necessary decision moving forward. He has a skill-set that helps them claim ownership, without embarrassment or guilt.

I have been in the multi-level, direct marketing, self-employed arena for over twenty-years. Over these last five months, as a direct result of becoming a member of the ATS University, I have started some new deals, restructured some old deals and completed and set aside some sweet deals. I'm not only learning about business in general, I'm learning about my business/es. I'm learning about Jerome Redd and Jerome Redd in real business. I am learning who he is. I am learning what he was. I am learning who he is becoming and I love every minute of it. Because poetry is another form of how I express myself, I had no choice in the matter. I had to write a poem about how I met Antonio T. Smith Jr. I hope you like it. It's called "I Wasn't Ready" I have attached a copy. I believe that it tells the story, better than my chapter.

I have to make one disclaimer and this is very important. As a poet, when I write a poem for someone, it is their poem, not mine. I just got the pleasure of writing it. So, in this case, I didn't copyright this poem. I gave it directly to Antonio.

I Wasn't Ready
(Caused By Antonio T. Smith Jr.)

I thought everything good. Well at least, that's what I told my man. But there were some rumblings going on, that I did not understand.

I was focused on my objective; a written Foreword by the, Les Brown. While distracted in my pursuit, I was unaware of what else was going down.

I succeeded and I was determined, and made contact, did I not mention? And while doggedly engaged for consent, I had drawn the likes of someone else's attention.

From his presentation, he knew his audience and he also, knew their needs. He gave enough to get their attention, so he could later bring them, up to speed.

So, in my pursuit to come on board, I attempted to verify that he was sharp. Only to find that he had targeted, exposed, empowered me, and pierced me right in my heart.

Talk about flipping the script, I was left

daze and very confused. When he uttered these powerful words, "What is it that I can do for you?"

I was silent and I was speechless. I did a double-take, and I was stunned.

I can't explain what had just taken place, but I knew that he was the one. This question is what I've said to so many, as I was reflecting on my past.

I didn't have his business card, address or phone number, but I knew this meeting would not be our last. I told him just what I needed, and he promised to keep me informed.

Something told that he's not like the others. There's no need for me to be scared or for warned.

So, he not only kept, but exceeded my expectations, if I didn't tell you, then I'd be a mist. If you want more than you can ask or desire, you need to hook up with Antonio T. Smith.

By Jerome Redd
August 23, 2018

Dr Patrick Businge

Clarity
Michelle L Mueller

53

Founder of One Red Shoe Foundation

You Gave Me Clarity

Dear Antonio,

I didn't know what to think when I first met you in person. I had watched you on social media, Bible study to be exact. I joined your church because you were different, you gave me clarity where I didn't even know there was fog. You answered questions that I didn't have a chance to ask. There was something about you that just pulled me towards you Maybe it was your past of being abandoned as a young boy at the age of 6, and I felt abandoned by my family at the age of 12.

We had different circumstances and very different cultures but we had a common bond. Both of us suffered sexual abuse. Both of us had been homeless for many years, you as a child, me as an adult. We both knew how it felt to be hungry, that painful empty ache, deep in your belly; hungry. The difference between us was...You had healed from your past, I had not. I remember telling you that I wanted more out of life, but I didn't know what. I just knew I wanted more of... something. I don't know if you took that as a challenge, or a victory.

If you ask me, I think I proved to be quite a challenge. At the age of 48, I was still blaming everyone else for my past. I was verbal about hating them while I was silently still hating me. You taught me how easy it was to forgive others. "Forgive like you did when you were 7 years old", you told me. It worked. Not only did you support me when I told you I had a nonprofit foundation but you were teaching me how to expand it. I remember when I had my first event. You encouraged me to tell my whole story and I shared how dirty I felt from the things I have done in my past. Afterwards, you prayed so beautifully and you said that I was as clean as a fresh glass of water. I am not sure if I ever told you this but, that was the moment I had finally forgiven myself.

I became a student in your leadership class where you taught me how to give grace as it is always so freely given to me. To walk in a constant state of forgiveness towards others as it always given to me. That there is no right or wrong and to allow others to be exactly who they are, even if that means allowing them to be who they are…..over there. You teach about integrity and good character and lead by example, always giving grace and honesty with so much ease because you know no other way.

You always speak the truth no matter how unwelcoming it is. I may be your student but your wish is for me to become better than you. You told me that I deserve to have whatever it is I want in life and then you would teach me how. You are my mentor and while you are stretching me...I am rejecting you. You are patient and wait until I decide I am ready. You are always there, smiling while you wait. You know me better than I know myself and you understand my struggle.

Thank you for letting me figure it on my own and not spoiling my journey. Because of your teachings, I look forward to the peaks in my life and I grateful for the valleys. You taught me how to be grateful for everything that has happened in my past and that it was all for a purpose. My purpose. That there is abundance of prosperity in this world and that I am worthy to receive it, for it is my birthright. You say "we are all connected and that there is only one of us in the room." That statement right there has made me kinder, more loving and more aware of the people I have the honor of meeting and look forward to meeting in this lifetime. Each and every one of them are a piece of me as I am a piece of them. Treating them accordingly is THEIR birthright. That is the most important thing I have learned from you.

The most important thing I have seen you do, for you practice it every moment of every day. To give value without conditions because they deserve it, and more importantly... I have it, to give. You have taught me to how to recognize my gifts and how operating in them will help me become the best version of me. I embrace my weaknesses and love every single thing about me. ...the good and the not so good. I have no limits because you are limitless, you let me borrow your faith when mine is absent. You showed me how to leap and keep flying and that the unknown isn't really scary at all, it is just a little uncomfortable. I think of you as "not so human" and I have told you so. You chuckle and are humble, just as I imagine a wise mine would do.

You have taught me about business and how to be a successful business woman. I now know how to communicate from my heart with the people I serve. I now believe, there is an abundance out there of anything that I want, there will always be enough, there is no lack. You taught me to expect greatness and to not settle for mediocrity.

I still have much to learn from you. Today I am hungry but it isn't that painful hurt deep down in my belly anymore. It is a pleasant hunger of wanting that takes place in my mind and in my heart. My mind wants to know more and do more, and my heart just wants to forgive and love more.

Thank you Antonio T Smith Jr, not only have you changed my life.....you saved my life. I used to be a career drug addict and prostitute. TODAY I am a CEO and Founder of the One Red Shoe Foundation and my mission is "There are No Spare women." I am a Les Brown certified speaker, trainer and coach. Currently, I hold the position of Director of Member Services and Director of Outreach at ATSJR Companies. I continue my outreach efforts in the streets of Galveston, TX, where I am making an impact on the women who live on them. I teach these women the same things Antonio taught me: They are worthy.

Confirmed
Dr Ira Roach III

America's Leadership Expert
www.driraroachiii.com

Confirmed

I was at my rock bottom in September of 2017, with a no show at my very first seminar after revamping my business. I joined the Les Brown Institute in October of 2017 and was excited about how this could fill all of gaps that I felt I was missing. It was December of 2017 and I was experiencing some issues with my Les Brown Institute courses. I reached out and a gentleman by the name of Antonio T Smith responded.

He walked me through the steps and changed my membership to enable me to enrol in all of the courses. Even after the initial meeting, I still ran into a few problems and was unable to access the courses that I had completed! I thought oh no, I won't get credit and won't be able to be certified at the April 2018 event. Once again, I reached out to Antonio and he was very pleasant and assisted me again. This time he told me not to worry about a thing and get my plane ticket for the Certification!

I finally arrived at the Certification in April 2018 and I wanted to meet Les Brown but I also wanted to meet this Antonio Smith Jr. This man helped me navigate through my issues with the website, gave me information and even, inspired me in less than 4 months. I had to meet him too! I was so excited to see that Antonio was one of the break out session presenters and I had to sign up for his workshop.

His session was entitled, "How to make six figures in your first year of speaking." I was literally blown away by the information that was given in the session. I also loved the confidence that exuded from this man. I remember him saying that he had an agenda but then said he would just do question and answer but he would only give a "millionaire" response. We went around the room and exchanged business cards and networked! I ran into him later after our sessions and he was down to earth and sat at a table and dropped knowledge again. I was just like a sponge soaking it all up!

Fast forward to July 2018, his team reached out and Antonio wanted me to interview with him. Once again, he asked me to throw any questions at him that I might have. By the end of the call this man had created opportunities for me that I never realized was inside of me. He gave me challenges such as Facebook lives on a subject which can lead to a product! He also affirmed my speaking career as a talk show host online! This blew me out of the water because I have always been insecure about my voice, but Antonio brought a description that caused me to have a different perspective about me!

That is who he is: a man that brings out the millionaire in you! I appreciate the coaching, training and the wisdom that I have received from being in the presence of Antonio T Smith Jr. Thank you for confirming my dream of becoming great!

Dominate
Chantelle Thompson

Transformational Speaker and Life Coach

64

Dominate

Chantell is the founder of Thompsons Worth LLC. She speaks internationally sharing her knowledge and compassion as a business owner and leader in her profession. She won a Les Brown Speakers Award in 2018 and partnered with the Les Brown Unlimited Team. By creating programs and keynote speeches, Chantell serves young people who battle with challenges that hinder their growth. This is after her experience of allowing hardships control her life and letting bad decisions define her. She is now eager to increase the awareness of oneself, help people pursue the power they have so that they can create the life they deserve. Here is her story on how Antonio Smith changed her life.

In 2017, I decided to pursue my dreams and build a business in transformational speaking, life coaching, and training. This was the start of something new, which called for an improved mind, body and soul. Once I was definite and focused on this decision, doors started opening up to receive the training, knowledge, and guidance I needed to get ahead in this passionate profession. Not knowing how or what to do, I began entering anything presented in front of me, spending energy, determination, and time on many people and information that was of value. However, this left me overwhelmed and running from the business I thought I wanted.

Once upon a time this was me, investing in mentor

after mentor, coach after coach, book after book, starting and never finishing any projects, and feeling alone in the business world.

In the midst of this, came along an opportunity that I haven't looked back from: the ATS Business University established by Antonio T Smith Jr. In June 2018, I joined this legacy and within 3 months, my mindset and business has been completely transformed. Now I understand what I desire, how to create it, and how to build revenue from it. Something I realized while investing in these previous trainings was that I continuously gave attention to people, places, and things that did not add value to my dreams. I was leaving my creativity inside to me and not expressing it to the world. I was telling myself that I was a procrastinator and lacked self-discipline. All this was blocking me from stepping into the boss that I am.

Craving to become a product of my own success but not seeing it transform, left me feeling disappointed in myself. Knowing you have a light flickering inside waiting to be set off into the world yet knowing it hasn't, can be very discouraging. Being blessed to become a part of Antonio's family and being a part of the action filled coaching classes, I have quickly been able to focus on who I am in this world. I have really grown and out of this grew the foundation of my business.

The ATS Business University that Antonio has built really makes me excited to go after my dreams. The interaction that I receive makes me feel connected with achievement driven people. I have experienced breakthroughs, tears, laughter, and joy while working with this team. I have been able to grow personally and physically when it comes to my business. I love Antonio and his team. This movement is legendary and I promise nothing like I have ever invested in before. Antonio is truly a man of his company. His vision, mission and purpose pours through in every training and live content he gives.

We as people striving for success in life, business and the world, want to be taught from a place where we are heard. We do not just want work or curriculum thrown at us with no personal connection to our real lives. Facts and research are beneficial but when entering the business world or looking to evolve into bigger and better, you want to feel supported and I know Antonio is dedicated to listening, understanding and supporting the curiosity of each person he works with. The proof is in each interaction with Antonio.

The consistency that Antonio and his team have shown me makes me know I am part of a family. The support and compassion for myself and each individual part of this family is undeniable and makes the accomplishments liberating and the adversity so easy get through. Embarking on this journey, I developed a fearless mindset, and this led me to making a decision of leaving an environment of poverty and traveling across the country into the unknown forcing me to live in wealth.

The university had belief in me that I did not have within me. Antonio and his team's genuine love made my experience so smooth and clear. Without the back up from the ATS Business University, I wonder how far I would have gotten. The information my ambassador gave me while introducing me to the company was great but what I have gained and learned these past 3 months has exceeded my expectations.

Before being apart of Antonio's legacy, my vision was unclear, my goals were scattered, and most of all I was lost on my journey. Now, not only have I learned how to set priority goals but I have learned how to make money within hours. I have built content quicker than I make a meal and made it profitable. The best part of it all, I am able to report back to a team which is supportive and ready to guide me to my next best step. My dreams are being created right before my eyes. All that I desire within is being heard and guided right into my reality. It is truly a dream come true.

I am a spontaneous, funny and risk taker. With this personality, my mind is always going and ready for action. Miraculously my needs are met and each week there are always solutions to the challenges presented to me in a simple practical way where I am able to achieve my goals. Needless to say, Antonio has changed my life and I look forward to being part of whatever he is part of. His heart is big and he is dedicated to changing lives and money cannot replace that.

A small message from me to Antonio T. Smith Jr, what you have envisioned is coming to light. Each day it is getting clearer and clearer. Your long sleepless nights are in the product of whatever has your name on it and you are dominating. Thank you for following your heart and going after what you knew you could be successful in. Without you, where would I be? Words become indescribable when expressing the way something makes you feel. My experience has been more than success it has been the start to the rest of my successful life. When you are excited and pumped to join trainings throughout the week, and I am talking enough to fill up each day of your week, you know you are part of something you love and that I am.

Dr Patrick Businge

Encouraged
M. Billye Sankofa Waters, Ph.D.

Associate Teaching Professor and Founding Executive Director of Blackgirl Gold Unapologetic, Inc. – NFP

www.drsankofawaters.com
www.blackgirlgold.org

Encouraged

To say that I have known Antonio all of his life is a bit of a misnomer. We are only a couple years apart. However, I can say that I have *loved* him his whole life. He was younger and shorter, which made him seem even younger and made me more inclined to protect him rather than hit and torture him like the rest of my boy cousins. We spent intermittent summers and holidays together between Galveston, Chicago, and that one time in Disney World when Antonio held him in his arms and carried through the admissions turnstile pretending he was a year younger, so he could get in for free. Ah the 80's!

I remember, nights he would have bad dreams and Linda would cuddle him as he cried in his sleep. That's the gift of being a couple years older; I have memories he may not have, and I know that he is always been protected by love. The Tony – or Antonio – that has been introduced to the world, is not the one I watched grow like a favorite tree in the backyard, only to have it stretch and pull and later cover you. I have walked along the Seawall with him as he spit his latest bars and I have recorded countless hours of (now buried!) video documenting him as *Paypa the Ghost* with other cousins and family friends. I remember the first time he put one of CDs in my hand – we were sitting in his car listening to the tracks and he told me about tours and dreams.

I have listened as he talked about losing his

grandmother/my aunt who had become the long-suffering matriarch for our family; periods of homelessness; and forgiving Anthony and Linda. I have watched him in the background as he dated and became a husband and a father; stood in the back of the church as he preached; debated in living rooms about theology and economics and Black liberation. I have been a front row witness to him walk into manhood – not simply by age but through patient intention.

Antonio is an incredibly private person, but he freely shares his narrative of light and 'silver linings.' His warmth makes you feel like there is no time or secret between you and that takes tremendous support, vision, confidence, and daily surrender. I am consistently encouraged by his choices to live life as a vessel to serve. More than that, I am honored to publicly share my experiences with him and the absolute joy of watching him grow from being my little knot-head cousin into a beautiful family man who confidently walks in abundance.

With Love and Light,

M. Billye Sankofa Waters, Ph.D.

Gifted
Todd Speciale

Founder of Omnigroup Global
www.ToddSpeciale.com

Gifted

I sat here for hours wondering where to start when it comes to Antonio. Was it the first time I met him at a Les Brown speaker event when he spoke to the entire crowd about how important his team was? That they were family and he incurred the cost so they can grow with or without him!? Or maybe it was that weekend, when he knew my father wasn't doing well. He saw it in my eyes and offered complete support without hesitation because he saw it in my eyes that I was hurting, even though we'd never met? Maybe it's the countless times he's noticeably put himself aside for others to rise, especially for me ANYTIME I have asked for his help with something. He never hesitated then and he doesn't hesitate now.

Maybe it his passion for believing in everyone so much, that if they win, he's happier than if he himself won! Maybe it's listening to him speak and getting chills as his voice inflection changes dramatically and touches your soul and every word he speaks he is able to make you feel as if it is exactly you he is talking to. Maybe it is the unwavering faith in God and his ability to give without expecting anything in return. Maybe it is how he built a multi-million dollar company and defied odds when others doubted him! Or maybe, it is his heart and how he somehow feels what you are feeling, as he uses his gift from above to somehow feel as if he is known you for a thousand years.....

I could go on and on and on, because every instance above Antonio has made possible in my life. He has been there for me whenever and however I have needed him. He has never said the word "no" to me. He challenged me to rise above the negativity, the voices of the haters, the naysayers, and helped me recognize the power I had to touch lives. He has given me strength when I felt weaker than I have ever felt and demanded I move forward pulling me like the leader he is paving the way never giving up on me.

Antonio is a gift from above. The calibre of person not many ever have the luxury of meeting in their lives. I personally have to thank him for the efforts, dedication, loyalty in life and love as my brother inspiring me to always be the best version of who I am. He has shared his tools of success just simply to see me grow.

You want to know who Antonio Smith Jr is? He is everything and more than any of us are worthy of having in one person! He is the type of guy who demands you to act on every day as if it is your last with full conviction. He is the guy who is not afraid to call you out and make you stand up when you are tired and sitting down. He is the man who has elevated me to levels only few reach and did it with zero expectations in return.

He pulled me aside one day and said, "At one point in your life, you have to get rid of the toxic people that are holding you back and simply allow yourself to become more." This was something that resonated deep within my soul for a couple of reasons. One, he did not even know that I was having some issues with people in my life at the time and was struggling on how to handle things. The second was his conviction when he speaks. He commanded my attention and it was like I had no other choice but to just listen. See, Antonio doesn't expect people to fail. He doesn't believe in failure and won't allow you to either.

When you have the chance to learn from a genius like this man, you just accept, shut up and listen. I do not trust people ever, but I trust him. I do not believe in people when they say they are going to do something, but he has ALWAYS come through. I do not jump when people say jump, but if he asks me to, I will. The complete dedication he gives to so many is so rare, that just being in his presence you feel you have already elevated your game. This man gave me some many business ideas that I still use to this day! He has never left my side. He speaks from his soul directly into your heart and lives what he preaches.

I will say this. In life you have two distinct differences in people, the ones who accept any challenges head on and the ones who run scared of what comes next. Antonio simply defies the odds. There is not a challenge he won't attack and handles adversity as if it were child's play. That type of will power cannot be taught, very rarely duplicated, but a gift for us all to see and knowing that ANYTHING is possible. I won't live my life without taking what I have learned from this man and implementing it in everything I do.

Most people do things for a personal gain. Antonio does it to watch those around him RISE! It is what makes him so unique. He would rather see the ones he has mentored and taught go to levels well above his own success and he is with you every step of the way holding you up, so you can keep climbing when you are starting to fall.

Antonio, we have our saying and I'm hoping we always will. We ask each other this question? "Have I ever said no to you?" And our answer is always "Nope, you never said no!" I will always have your back, I am thankful for having you in my time of need in every aspect of my life, but MOST IMPORTANTLY your genuine ability to make me feel like family, not just friends. You are one of the best businessmen I have ever known and without you, I am not sure where I would be. Shine on brother, you deserve to live for eternity. The world needs in it forever!

Giver

Shannon Clark

Transformational Coach and Director of Counseling

Giver

Shannon empowers people to see the promise hidden in their pain, the glory buried in their gut and the work required of their mind. She is a Les Brown certified speaker, trainer and coach. She is employed by The Antonio T. Smith Jr. Companies as a Transformational Coach as well as the Director of Counseling. She holds a Bachelor of Science degree in Psychology from the University of Houston and two Master degrees in Counseling and Education Administration from Prairie View A&M University. She is the mother of one and enjoys reading, speaking and empowering others see the greatness they possess within them. Here is her story on how Antonio Smith changed her life.

A victim of childhood sexual abuse and domestic violence, a single mother of one working tirelessly to provide for her son and deeply rooted in a belief system that did not serve me, I was suffering. This coupled with extreme arrogance; one could imagine I was one tough cookie upon meeting Antonio T. Smith Jr. When I met him, Antonio was everything I thought I wanted to remain far away from: A young and loud Baptist preacher. I wanted no parts. I immediately figured I knew everything I needed to know. Luckily, I really liked his administrative assistant at the time, Tempestt, and because she vouched for him, I purchased his book *Keep Walking*. This book allowed me to let down my guard and see what this guy was all about and I am glad I did.

I would have never imagined the journey Antonio had taken to accomplish all that he had amassed at this point in his life. Antonio and his church became some of my most genuine and faithful supporters in our denominational church work and it was in one meeting in particular I decided, if offered, I would consider working with him. We had just concluded this meeting and someone close to him asked for prayer. They said they had quit their place of employment to work for Antonio full-time because they trusted him and believed in what he wanted to do to impact the world. Today, approximately six years later, that person is a millionaire.

Antonio did not put me to work immediately, as my character could not sustain the culture of his company. Remember, I was suffering. I was living a life that was relentlessly devoted to pleasing and serving others perpetually so that I could not please and serve myself authentically. I was walking dead. Even more unsettling, I was perfectly fine with this existence; I welcomed the pain, the frustration, the sadness, the control, and the idolization. I needed work and Antonio knew it more in-depth than I did, unbeknownst to me at the time.

Instead of employing me, he offered me a seat in his coveted Integrity Leadership course. Antonio offered this at no charge provided I would vow not to ever miss his class. This ten-month leadership class inaugurated a culture of evolution and awareness in my life that I honestly believe I will never be able to repay him for. Antonio lectured tirelessly every Wednesday evening for two hours or more building character, raising consciousness and changing lives. For the first half of the course, I received nothing. I would purposely close my mind to the teachings, choosing instead to watch Antonio and wait for him to fail me. In my mind, he could not be as smart and giving as he was without a divine flaw. He remained the same, even when I threw daggers, he responded with transparency, love and knowledge. Two months before the end of the class I 'unzipped', I let down my guard, I demolished the walls I had built around my mind and my heart. This would not have occurred without Antonio's teachings and support.

Upon completion of my first year of the Integrity Leadership course, Mr. Smith did two things: first, he employed me as an instructor, affording me the opportunity to teach a course on retraining the subconscious mind for his Plant Better University, which now serves as the Netflix of self-development. Second, he told me I had to take the course again. The first round was brutal however I did not want it to end. Needless to say, I was pleased to receive an invitation to take the course again. It was during this second season of the course that my layers peeled away and my true self emerged.

With this authentic self came a heightened level of awareness and a dramatic improvement in character.

I was now in a better mental state, able to detail what it was I desired in life. Through Antonio's teachings I learned I am a creator and anything I want I can have provided I create a system to obtain it.

Antonio did not stop here; he also invited me to join his personal mastermind team. He inquired about my dreams and asked that I give him a detailed list of all that I desired. Since the day that list hit his hand, he has worked to the point of death to ensure others and I receive all that we want. He told me he would die making sure my dreams lived; I didn't believe him until he showed me. I am not the only person he does this for, I am sure you have read similar accounts from others.

I am now in my third year of Antonio's Integrity Leadership Course, however I am not only a student but an occasional instructor. I am a student attending the ATS Business University, I am an instructor for Plant Better University, I am a transformational life coach and the Director of Counseling for The ATS Jr. Companies. I hold equity in one of his companies and all I invested was poor character and rejection. While my character has improved and I now receive all of his teachings I will never be able to compensate Antonio for all he's given me. Our team has become my family, my support system and my realm of accountability.

I never would have imagined this had I not encountered Antonio T. Smith Jr. We clash like rival siblings, I have challenged him on many instances and he has never changed, I have quit and he has welcomed me back with open arms and opportunity. He's never treated me anything less that worthy and has always given me an others his very best. He is everything he says he is and I am better today because I met him and most importantly, because I received him. He's a great guy. He is my boss and my friend. It is an honor to know him and a joy to be known by him. I love him dearly and there's nothing he can do about it.

Gratitude
Tempestt Smith

Entrepreneur, Speaker, Business Coach, and CEO of ATS Jr. Companies

Friendship is the hardest thing in the world to explain. It's not something you learn in school. But if you haven't learned the meaning of friendship, you really haven't learned anything.
- Muhammad Ali

Gratitude

Tempestt S. Smith joined ATS Jr. Companies before it was called its current name in 2011 to provide administrative support as a secretary. She immediately made a major impact and was promoted within a few months to Antonio T. Smith Jr.'s, personal assistant. Within a few years, the company would grow to having many assistants and volunteers and Tempestt would be promoted once more to Executive Assistant overseeing more than 54 people. Tempestt would be so efficient throughout the years to come that Antonio would offer her 30% ownership in most of his companies.

Today, Tempestt is not just an assistant, but a CEO. She has very strong skill sets in media production, including audio, film, television and radio, computer programming, to add to her administration talents. She has developed strong relationships with Lakewood Church of Houston, Texas, as well as top business firms and publication companies. She is also a Les Brown Certified Speaker, Trainer, and Coach, and can now add international trainer and keynote speaker to her accolades. She co-hosts the Brick By Brick podcast with Antonio, which reaches over 70 countries and has become known as a worldwide inspiration and hope to all who have been abused and introverts everywhere. Tempestt has founded companies on her own that operate within the umbrella of the ATS Jr Companies.

Tempestt is a public relations and strategic communications expert. She has worked in media, crisis communications, publishing, hospitality, church and technology. She has consulted for major church convention outlets and colleges and universities. Tempestt has also produced countless web documentaries and series with Antonio and is often one the creative minds and writers behind many things his audience has come to love. Here is her story on how Antonio Smith changed her life.

I met Antonio T. Smith Jr. in the summer of 2011. June 2011 to be exact. Actually, it was a Saturday, June 25, 2011 at around noon. I have a great memory but remembering exact dates and times I met people is not my gift, however, I remember this day because for me it was monumental. At this time, I was working front desk at a hotel in Houston. As I was working, and I had zero desire to be at work listening to hotel guests either complain without even acknowledging me or any of my coworkers.

As my shift began to slow down a bit, in walks a man with what I now jokingly call an entourage following him. As he and the crew walked towards the conference room where a meeting was getting ready to be held, I could not help but notice how confident he and those around him were. I was used to the Saturday network marketers. They were annoying, pushy and borderline cocky, but not him... or not as much. About 90 minutes later and after not so politely requesting my contact information, to show me a presentation of the network marketing company he was associated with at the time, he left and somehow, I knew that was not the end of any interactions with him. And the rest, as they say is history.

After my first real interaction with him, I learned that Antonio was definitely a leader. In fact, I have heard him tell plenty of people before how he is the leader that they are looking for. To be very honest, in 2011, I had no idea I wanted or needed a leader. I did not want anyone telling me what to do. In my mind, I was doing what I was supposed to do. Showing up for work and going to school. It wasn't until I met Antonio that I discovered that working and going to school were not the only things life had to offer. He showed me that I was missing life by doing the same thing that everyone else did and not doing what few are bold enough to do. I learnt how to allow myself to experience life. His leadership for me evolved into a mentorship, to a work relationship, business partnership, and ultimately an unbreakable bond that has withstood many test, storms and breaking moments.

As his now business partner, I could talk about how Antonio changed my life by surprising me while recording a podcast episode of how he was making me his business partner. He offered me a significant chunk of his entire empire and while that did and has drastically changed my life, that's not why I signed up. Antonio T. Smith Jr. changed my life by simply existing. After seven years and some change, it is an understatement to say I have learned a lot from him. From books, to conversations, to traveling all around the world, there is no doubt that I have been poured into by Antonio.

However, his pure existence changed me. When I first met him, he told me how he grew up homeless, how his mother and father abandoned him due to drug addictions. He told me how he had to sleep inside of a dumpster and has shown me the exact location where he lived. He told me how hard it was going to school, or trying to, as a homeless child who could not take baths, comb his hair or even have a pencil and a desk to do homework. But through all of this, he still manages to wear an incredibly huge smile. He taught me how to be grateful and this has been the ultimate lesson above all of the rest.

Growing up, I did not have a bad childhood. In fact, I felt it was very normal. Yes, my mother was a single parent with two children. No, my father was not around but my brother and I never went without basic necessities. Somehow, I knew my mother and/or my grandparents would make things work. Somewhere along the way, I knew about gratitude but failed to put it into an everyday practice. After learning about his childhood, I began to see how gratitude actually works. It's not saying, "thank you" or "I'm grateful" during the holiday season, but it is truly a practice.

Anyone who knows me knows that I have an absolute love for office supplies, pens, pencils, paper, notebooks, post-it's, etc. I love it all. I remember the first time I brought Antonio a box of mechanical pencils, his face lit up and a huge smile appeared on his face. For weeks, he talked about how grateful he was for a box of pencils. While, I too am always happy about such products, I never showed appreciation for them. Every time I saw him, he went into his pocket or inside of his backpack and showed me how many pencils he had left and how much he was taking care of the gift I purchased. Initially, I thought he was just being weird but every single time I purchased something for him, or shared something with him, he showed the exact reaction. Whether it was a pencil or food or a keychain, he showed genuine, heartfelt appreciation and gratitude for whatever it was.

Before there was an ATS Jr. Companies, there was Without An Umbrella Ministries. A ministry that Antonio started whose mission was to teach individuals that they can survive the storms of life, even without an umbrella. During the building stages of what is now all things ATS Jr. we struggled a lot. However, even in the struggle, Antonio was grateful. I on the other hand was not. When I had my first car repossessed, I was furious, crushed and felt like my world was spiraling out of control.

Antonio reminded me to pause, breathe, and remember that this was not the end of the world. I brushed him off because "he didn't understand." Not too long afterwards, his car was repossessed. I noticed he did not have the same reaction I did. Yes it bothered him but instead of wallowing like I did, he moved forward and told me that things happen and something greater was on its way. For me, "on the way" meant very soon, much better, faster but it didn't happen that way. "On the way" came in the form of a Ford Focus that he purchased and together, 60 miles away, we made one car work. With not enough money to eat a real meal, we often shared one bag of Doritos and two Arizona teas (they were $0.99 each) and every time I wanted, thought about or went to complain, I looked over to my passenger and saw, felt and heard the gratitude excluding from his pores and it made me realize that if someone who grew up homeless, in a dumpster, who had to constantly defend himself, withstand rain, heat, winds, hurricanes, cold weather, bugs, lack of food, lack of guidance, lack of love could show gratitude, certainly so could I.

Antonio T. Smith changed my life not by talking a good game, but living up to and exceeding what he taught. Without gratitude, we have nothing and I carry that valuable lesson with me every single day.

Integrity
Rev. Bryant Johnson

Church Minister

Integrity Class

Antonio T. Smith has forever changed my life. I met Antonio at a time in my life when I was dealing with church hurt from one religious organization and not getting paid my deserving worth while working at another religious organization.

Antonio and I met at a local Starbucks in Texas City, TX and before I could open my mouth and go on a tyrant about why I was feeling the way I was feeling, Antonio told me the Biblical story of David and King Saul. Upon finishing the story he looked at me and said, Rev., God will sit you under a King Saul to get rid of the King Saul in you. As much as I wanted to reject it, I received that message. This message itself began to change my mindset that eventually lead to a great change in my bank account.

Antonio is the epitome of a leader. His wisdom and his heart is a true example of why God sent Jesus to earth. Not only is Antonio good at helping you create financial security for yourself and your family but Antonio has a gift in teaching you about the importance of integrity and how to have the character to follow that integrity. Anger and unforgiveness was a major stumbling block for me. After meeting Antonio, I can now say that those character flaws are no longer holding me back from my purpose. Rest assured, I now can say I would not be at this level of success if I hadn't crossed paths with Antonio T. Smith Jr.

After that meeting at Starbucks that day, Antonio invited me to another meeting that was held on a Friday evening at a Panera Bread Restaurant in League City, TX. There I met the KodeInc Tech Team (Tempestt, Deaunna and Grace) which is Antonio web design company. I was invited to become part of that team working in the sales department with Grace Sandles and, also to work in the distribution side of Antonio's record label WAU Records. Being offered these two positions did something very beneficial for me. First, it allowed me the opportunity to be a part of a family that wants to see the best of me manifested into reality. It also offered me the opportunity to become a millionaire and leave the place where I was getting underpaid and underappreciated.

I didn't leave my place of employment that day but shortly thereafter the day would come. What helped me the most to be emotionally prepared for this day was I enrolled into Antonio's 40 week Integrity Class. While in this class, I learned that my feelings are why I keep getting the results that I was getting. The only thing I was manifesting are the feelings I put behind my dominant thoughts. Again this is thanks to Antonio.

I honestly, would not know anything about dominant thoughts without the Integrity Class. Me leaving a place that no longer served me would have been a catastrophe because I would have left leaving a stain of anger on the organization and not only was that not good for myself because of the title I held but it would not have been good for the organization as well. The Integrity Class not only changed my character, but it also changed my view of money. In all honesty I used to be scared to have a lot of money because I knew I lacked the financial intelligence to keep it or to utilize it in a manner to manifest my dreams.

One Saturday morning before our church service began, Antonio and Tempestt invited Deaunna and myself into the office to look at an evaluation of Brook Kerith University. Upon looking at the evaluation, tears began to flow from my eyes and gratitude filled my heart. The reason these emotions were flowing so heavily on me and I began speaking with the utterance of tongues (spiritual term) and giving praises to The Most High, because this evaluation had each person that invested in the University at a millionaire. That day was the icing on the cake for me to fully know that I was allowed to join the right team at the right time to put me in the right position to fulfill my dreams and live my purposeful life to help transform and change the world with the proper spiritual awareness I needed to live in abundance.

Living at the highest expression of ourselves is the greatest gift we can give ourselves while living this life here on this earth. Antonio surely lives at the highest expression of himself and it is raising higher daily. I watch Antonio not stress, not worry, nor get defeated easily and these are some things us as people do and do often. We easily fall victim to negativity and feel defeated when we don't put forth the energy nor effort to be successful. Antonio teaches you to raise your awareness level to understand what doesn't deserve you doesn't deserve your energy. One phrase he says, and I love to hear it, is. "Just because you are invited to an argument doesn't mean you have to join the party". This phrase is not just a phrase for arguments or debates, it's a phrase that I utilize to cover every area of my life. What does not serve me nor add value to me nor my life no longer needs to receive my attention nor energy. I recommend every one reading this to take this and make this your life motto!

And today I am The Double Certified Peoples Pastor. I have multiple degrees and millions of dollars and will be Pastoring The Brook Cherith Baptist Church (Church For the Unchurched) which is the church Antonio has founded and organized. I have achieved all this because of meeting, learning from and growing under the wings of The Millionaire Maker Mr. Antonio T Smith Jr.

King
Law Loadholt

Leadership Coach, Keynote Speaker,
Travel Vlogger

104

King

Law Loadholt is a Transformational Leadership Coach, Keynote Speaker, Travel Vlogger, and Founder & CEO of Launching With Law. With his system Master Your Choice, he shows his clients how to figure out their purpose in a world of endless opportunities. His mission is to change mindsets and elevate vision of self. Here is his story on how Antonio T. Smith Jr. changed his life.

I would often pray to God for a story to tell: a story that would give my life meaning and impact the lives of many. It was not enough that I was separated from my parents at a young age, experiencing the harsh realities of foster care and having sex at a young age.

God said, "Are you satisfied with your story now?" I replied, "It's not captivating enough". God responded, "Okay". At the age of 23, I experienced a mental breakdown that developed into panic disorder and agoraphobia. I spent 2 years trapped in mind, inside of home, unable to venture into the world. Then God asked me, "Is your story captivating enough?". My reply was, "Yes, I have more than enough story to tell".

I am one of eight children; but five of my siblings have experienced the world of foster care and we all have a different story. I am thankful that my mother came back for us! I was a child raising himself in foster care, bouncing from home to home. I was nothing more than check. There was no one teaching me right from wrong or forcing me to go to school. I can remember many hungry nights and no clean clothes. I would pray that the other foster children would not steal my shoes off my feet as I slept. Somehow there was always a light within in me that never dimmed. I would always look to the brighter side for I knew that this wouldn't be my reality forever!

I was separated from my mother at the age 3 because of drug abuse and my father ran off with his new wife. We spent about a year in foster care and custody was granted to my father. At this time, there was only four of us growing up in foster care and he could only provide for two children. The youngest two were placed back into foster care.

My father raised my brother and I for five years and then he placed us back into foster care. He dropped us off like trash in the night and he never said good bye. He chose his new wife over us his children. During this time, I still didn't know who my biological mother was and it was a process to reunite with her.

The Game

It was all a game! He said, "Let me show you a game that adults play." I played the game for a couple of years before a new kid came along and didn't want to play anymore. So what did I do? I taught someone else to play the game! I taught this game a few times, before I was taught kids do not play this game. I still remember that day embarrassing day in the therapist's office. "So, Lawrence your brother tells me that you guys play a special game?" Can you tell me about this game?

My little brother broke the rules, how could he? I always played by the rules and I never told. The therapist told me that children do not play these games. It took years for me to forgive myself. It took even longer to understand the changes in my mind and body. I had to replace the pleasure that was once taught with love.

Dope Head

At the age of 23, I became a Dope Head! No I wasn't the Kool Kid on the block or the junkie trying to the next fix. I was a zombie! They said, "this pill will make you feel happy. This one will help you sleep. This one will help you deal with life. This one will make you gain weight."

Let's not forget about the side effects: blurry vision, tremors like Parkinson Disease, muscle spasms (Hurry up and get to hospital before your body snaps your head off of your neck, because it continues to open and you have no control). I went in for a routine operation and came out with mental break down that developed into panic disorder and agoraphobia. Agoraphobia is a fear of crowds, situations, and the outside world. It was just a tonsillectomy and adenoidectomy. Yes, Mr. Doctor I cannot eat anything for one week, but why it is two weeks later and I am severely sick in hospital. I was unable to keep anything down, high fevers, cold chills, and night sweats. I had lots of questions to ask Mr. Doctor.

Mr. Doctor why did I go from a size 34 to 27 in two weeks? Mr. Doctor did you say the acid from my vomit is eroding the enamel in my teeth? Mr. Doctor why am I so frail and weak and have to walk with a cane at 23 years old? At this point in time, I could no longer get on the bus. I could no longer get on a train. I could no longer travel on the plane.

I spent two years trapped in my mind, inside of my house. Unable to venture into the world. But did you know that Law was an honor student? Law was a social butterfly. Law was a college graduate. Law completed his BBA in 3 years and a semester early. Law had a 3.6 GPA and worked a full time job as a manager at Starbucks. I even went to class during the day, at night, online, and partied like no tomorrow.

My student loans were paid off before I graduated. I was 21, with a nice car and no car note. I had an apartment and 20K in the bank. All of which was unheard of for a young black man from the hood.

Thank You ATS

My relationship with Antonio started off as a dress competition, that morphed into a beautiful mentorship. We would give each other props in passing at a Les Brown training event. I never knew who he was or what he represented. He seemed like a great guy who had a lot of swag. Low and behold he was millionaire speaker that loved my style. Talk about humbled!

When the training event concluded, Antonio asked me how can he stay in touch with me? He had a King hat on and he asked me, "What it meant?" I said, "It means me, I am King!" Antonio tossed the hat to me and it has been on my shelf ever since. Before I knew it, I was calling him for advice on what to do next to grow my brand and elevate my speaking abilities. Antonio asked me two important questions. He first asked me, 'What makes your heart hurt?'. I replied, 'complacency'. I was looking at the disorder in my dining room and it made no sense that my house was in a disarray with seven adults. He then asked me, 'What are you willing to die for?' I replied, I will to die for my nephew. My nephew is splitting image of me and we have similar personalities. I am always reminding him that he can do and be anything that he wants in life.

Antonio instructed me to do 30 days of Facebook lives on the topic of complacency. Every day I would speak for 30-60 minutes on 12 signs that you are living a complacent life, how to overcome those 12 signs, and how to release complacency in personal and intimate relationships. This idea gave birth to the Releasing Complacency Training Course, my first book, and it made me a better speaker. With the help of Antonio and his team, I am making headways in the speaking industry.

Mentored
Malisa Thomas

Mentored

I met Antonio approximately 10 years ago when he was about to retire as a manager. I was immediately intrigued as to how this young husband and father was retiring so young from corporate America. I knew then, whatever he was doing I was going to do. One of the many things I observe about Antonio is that as he grows, he grows other. He knows that in life there is more than enough for everyone. Antonio T. Smith Jr. has always been a rarity- a diamond from the moment I met him, he began pouring into my life on many levels. Antonio T. Smith Jr. has been my brother, my pastor, my mentor and best of my friend.

In approximately 2011, I wrote my first skit for church. The gentleman that was supposed to play my husband backed out in the last hour- fourth quarter before we were set to go on stage. I called my brother Antonio Smith Jr. and like a true brother Antonio dropped what he was doing and memorized the part and played my husband. He truly is his sister's keeper.

On 15th June 2017, I was 3 months pregnant and I received less than favorable test results. The lab was unable to rule out a chromosomal defect with my child. I reached out to Antonio while he was setting up for a Galveston County Event. Antonio responded with a list of healing scriptures and then he said, "Pay very close attention to what I say next, concerning the LAW OF ATTRACTION AND HEALING YOUR CHILD." You must accept some basic points:

- ✓ It is natural for your child to be well

- ✓ Your child really does know what to do to heal itself

- ✓ Don't waste your precious mental energy figuring out how it happened

- ✓ You don't need to understand the illness for it doesn't matter in the healing process

- ✓ Your only concern is to align yourself with your natural state of wellness and concentrate on the healing.

After hearing these words from Antonio, I no longer felt sad and depressed. I felt as though there was hope. Antonio went on to walked me through the law of attraction and what he did when he was in my situation. Antonio told me,

> The first thing to do, as in any purposeful use of the law of attraction, is to be absolutely clear in what you want. Take the time to paint a vivid mental picture of your kid in the best of health, completely healed, totally healthy and happy. This is so important! You must include feelings of being healthy in your picture. Create an in-mind video of joyfully running with the

children, playing in a field, working out at the gym, walking down the road. Feel what healthy breathing feels like, what your healthy body feels like and see your kid this way. The more vivid you can make this image in your mind, the faster the healing process will happen.

I prayed, followed his instructions and worked to control my thoughts. My son was born healthy in December 6, 2017. That's Antonio Smith Jr my pastor.

Antonio Smith Jr is my life mentor. Antonio Smith Jr selflessly pours his wisdom and expertise in my life and others. Antonio Smith Jr has a sincere desire to help others. When I went to Antonio's home many years ago, he had post it notes of quotes all over the bathroom. The quotes were mindset changing. Whenever I think of the quote by Gandhi "Be the change that you wish to see in the world", I think of Antonio and his actions. He is living out Gandhi's words. Because of his actions I am transparent with him and share my dreams. He has incorporated my goals into his future plans.

A friend gives good advice, has a sincere interest in your life and great influencer. Antonio Smith Jr my friend, once made a promise not to me but to Our Father in Heaven. Antonio said, "I promise To Our Father I will be a major blessing to you and your family". My friend, does not just have an interest in me, he is interested and want the best for my family too. My desires are his desires for me and that is a true friend. That's the Antonio Smith Jr I love and respect and truly value.

Antonio T. Smith Jr. changed my life, by changing my mind, helped me create a vision and reminded me all things are possible through Christ.

Possibility
B J Fletcher

Dr Patrick Businge

Possibility

Antonio T. Smith Jr. is a character, a person, and individual who stood on the corner of a very important turning point in my life. Up until that point, I was traveling down a very dark and lonely road. When I looked up, I saw Antonio standing there but he was standing out; like a bright shining billboard.

When I first met Antonio, there was an instant connection. When we first spoke, his entire being sent a message to my heart and mind of reassured faith in my capabilities. I could automatically tell that we had several similarities. He was a Southern black man close to my age. He was active in the ministry. He is a former athlete. He has military ties. He is a father. I discovered that we have had many parallel life experiences. While our lifestyles might not be exactly the same, without a doubt, we are very similar breeds. Our breeds are so similar that it led me to believe that he understands my struggles, my vices, and my aspirations, tacitly. It's very encouraging feeling to know somebody who can relate to what you are, but it's inspiring to see that they have put themselves in positions to navigate into higher levels of success.

I innately understood that Antonio had the ability and insight to help escort me though my current situation towards some of the wonderful possibilities I had imagined. The possibilities that will set me up for some the great things I desire. He revealed to me that they are great possibilities for our type. Then he offered me an opportunity to work with him as my coach. At first, I wouldn't jump on as his coaching client, I thought that he'd make a better friend than a coach because we had so many similarities. But after several conversations I signed up for his coaching because I believed in what he saw in me.

I can be very critical on coaches. I maybe even somewhat difficult to coach. I often liken coaches to multivitamins because almost every coach has certain insights and philosophies that they say will lead a person to success. Just like almost every multivitamin has certain vitamins and minerals that companies claim will help a person reach optimal health. But the quality of both a coach and a multivitamin are determined by how much of the "good stuff" gets absorbed. If it's a multivitamin, how many of those vitamins and minerals are getting digested and added to the bloodstream? If it's a coach, how much of your insights and philosophy is comprehended and applicable enough to be put into practice? This is just my measuring stick and how I can fairly appraise coaches and multivitamins and their potential capacity to be beneficial or life-changing.

I believe the most difficult part of coaching is finding clients that are coachable. Being a coachable client is the ability to digest or comprehend the messages that the coach is trying to convey. The order for a client to begin to be coachable. A coach must be believable.

There are several factors that play into the believability of a coach, depending upon a client's situation and their position in life. So, in order for a coach to seem believable to me, they must be able to display the competency needed to navigate through my current position in life and beyond.

I like to relate almost everything in life to sports. In the game of football, every player has position coaches. A position coach is someone who focuses on your current position then teaches you how to maneuver yourself into better situations successful. Position coaches are usually not the only coach you work with but because of all the intimacy required for your growth & development, they tend to be the coaches with whom you cultivate the closet bonds. That's one of the things I like about Antonio. He has a gift for developing close relationships. That is what let me allow him to help me change my life.

I say allow because in any coaching relationship there must be a mutual agreement of honesty, integrity, trust, and progression. Everyone needs a cheerleader, someone to support, encourage, and reassure them. But a great coach not only helps their players realize just how special they are, how much they deserve and how much more they can be, great coaches also help players recognize and accept accountability for the part they are playing in their own success.

Antonio played his part. He is a great coach to me. Every time we came in contact with each other we had a special greeting. It was a big to do. We'd both act like announcers at a big event calling out stars name. I would straighten up and stand tall and with a deep voice say Antonio… T… Smith… Jr, like I was announcing the president at his State of The Union Address. He'd take a slight pause for the applause then would say: B…J… Fletcher!!!! then makes sounds like the crowd was going wild. We'd both flash huge smiles and give each other big bro hugs.

It became a regular habit for us to celebrate each other. We were also open and honest enough to give real constructive criticisms. When we have had in-depth conversations about our backgrounds, accomplishments, current goals: I can count on Antonio to point out contradictions between my intentions and actions. Which is something that is very hard for an individual to do by themselves. Because "it's hard to see the picture when you in the frame".

I could go on and on describing the details of how Antonio has helped me change my life. I could tell stories of the amazing things we have experienced together or his use and practice of group economics: Something that I only knew of in theory and never saw practiced. Or I could talk about his leadership abilities. How he plots, plans, and gathers crowds of supporters. The three things that separate those brilliant minds from being historical figures.

But the one thing stands out is how Antonio has helped me change my life the most is without a doubt his encouragement. He has a special brand of encouragement that is hard to describe. Is something that you must experience to understand. He really knows how to walk the line. He is encouraging without being too pushy. He is pushy without being repulsive. He is involved without being invasive. The things he says and ideas he presents resonates in my mind for days, weeks and even months after we speak.

The only thing that I could compare that to is a position coach. That's how Antonio T Smith Jr has changed my life. He has been my position coach, helping me know for myself that situation successfully this game called life.

Renewed
Michael Tate

Entrepreneur

www.optimizeyourcredit.com

Dr Patrick Businge

Renewed

Michael Tate is the co-founder of Creditology LLC: a national credit restoration and financial literacy firm. It focuses on building business and consumer credit profiles and offers business loans and key person life insurance to protect personal and business assets. Here is his story on how Antonio changed his life.

Making the introduction

I met Antonio and the ATS Business University staff at a training seminar in April 2018. The host city was Fort Lauderdale, Florida and the event was powerful and informative. My primary ambition was to fly to Florida, learn how to become a better professional speaker and hopefully, meet influential people in the process. Though internally that was my plan, I was not going out of my way to execute it. Candidly, I was excited to meet other successful motivational speakers and have the opportunity to snap a photo or two with them. As I did this, I was thinking to myself "all of these self-help seminars are the same." Typically you have a well-known guest/speaker who speaks about consistent strategies and tactics, get the crowd "hype" then make a compelling, yet emotional call to action that sounds something like this, "If this is your purpose in life and you believe you can do what I do by reaching millions of people with your personal message, sign here on the dotted line and allow us to deduct a payment from your account the size of a second mortgage."

To my chagrin, there was a call to action, which I expected and I, like the others in attendance, I was moved instantly with such vigor and charm. Fortunately for me, I snapped out of the trance when an announcement was made that there would be "breakout sessions" during the seminar. The sessions were optional, but gave other speakers, both seasoned and upcoming, the opportunity to make a personal connection with the audience and subsequently, make an offer for their products and services. Being a sales executive for more than 20 years this was expected and appreciated, but I was convinced it was not for me. I would not be making an investment with anyone during my short, yet beautiful stay in Florida. Boy, was I wrong.

Creating value

Day two of the training seminar and the mental exhaustion associated with listening to multiple speakers back to back with limited breaks was wearing me down. Although the variations of content were relevant and often entertaining, I needed more stimuli and time to retain the new information I learned. When the music came on and the announcement was made that it was time for a breakout session, I broke out the conference room like a prisoner from the state penitentiary and headed out to find other like minds to make meaningful connections. I did not have one person in mind when I left the room to network, but I was looking for someone who was relatable, honest, knowledgeable, and successful at what they do, an expert in their niche.

I spent some time vetting others to assess their knowledge, skills, abilities and qualifications. I also observed the crowd and engaged in a little bit of people watching. I pondered over what I needed most from this event and derived at the conclusion that I would benefit most from having a business coach to help me streamline operational costs, enhance online marketing, and hold me accountable with my business productivity and financial goals.

The first breakout session was with a professional salesperson who touted his many accomplishments and spent more time convincing the crowd that he was successful and had all the answers versus speaking to how he can help the audience achieve success. I attentively listened and awaited for the sales pitch but was anxiously wanting the session to be over so that I could continue my search for a business coach. Reluctant to attend additional breakout sessions, I scoured a few of the smaller conference rooms and walked into a session on "How to Make a $1M Dollars in a Year." The session title caught my attention but for some reason, this session felt different from the previous sessions.

Becoming a part of the team

As I entered the room, I was impressed that there were no seats available, standing room only. The room was electrifying. An ATS Business University team member, later I would know as Michelle, the university's onboarding ambassador, made an unselfish offer of extending her chair to me. As a southern gentleman, I initially refused, but she insisted and I confirmed and accepted her offer. The team's energy was contagious and I became eager to explore if the speaker was going to be more of the same that I already heard or was he going to offer any new relevant information.

I noticed there was a young man dressed in a black designer suit, no tie and t-shirt with the face of a lion on it and the letters ATS written across the top. After sharing a brief introduction of himself, the team and their successes, he stood there in front of the crowd and told the audience that he was prepared to discuss a certain topic, but was calling an audible to address the specific needs of the audience. My first thought was "Huh, what does that mean?" I stood there silently wondering if this this was a sales Jedi mind trick/tactic I had not been exposed to before. As I continued to listen, I was skeptical. I crossed my arms squinted my eyes and waited for the scam to reveal itself.

Antonio's statement prompted many specific questions from the audience. I waited attentively for his rebuttals and to my surprise he fired back with sharp, relevant and innovate responses. I then tenaciously decided to participate in the group dialogue and asked a question about online Facebook marketing. His entrepreneurial response resonated with me immediately, but I still was not convinced he was the answer to what I was looking for.

After the session, I stood in line among others to get a close up, to introduce myself and to personalized a potential networking opportunity with a successful person. When I made it to the front of the line, he did it again. He was very personable, approachable, charismatic, and witty. I left that brief introduction thinking to myself, "This investment was worth the risk." Good solid and relevant information was shared, the environment was conducive, the staff was pleasant, and their company headquarters is located in Galveston, TX which is only 52 minutes from my home. In that moment, I made the decision to become yet another ATS Business University millionaire!

The turning point

As I exited the room, I felt renewed and invigorated. I had a new-found belief that the ATS Business University was going to help me turn my ship around. I began looking for a team member to enroll me into the university and was greeted by Pastor Bryant Johnson, whom I met briefly the first day of the training session where we shared the same dinner table and exchanged pleasantries. I immediately believed this was celestial confirmation and immediately enrolled into the university. After making this enrollment decision, I instantly knew it would yield results. I immediately regained the confidence in myself and believed this was the business coach I needed to take me to the next level.

Since meeting Antonio in April 2018, I have:
- ✓ Revitalized my company's website and business plan
- ✓ Increased my online presence through videos/advertisements
- ✓ Increased client acquisitions
- ✓ Participated in multiple ATS business coaching & training calls.

I am an official member of the ATS team. I have partnered with other ATS affiliates to deliver financial advice. I am Antonio's personal Financial Advisor and I lend my experience and resources to the ATS University as well. The professional aspect of my business has turned around completely. I have made time to focus on the things that are the most important to me. By putting first things first, my family has recognized the changes in my thought process and actions. Most importantly, I see and feel the changes happening to me and within me.

Rescued
Aisha Tetubatya

Founder of Showtime Century Movies

Rescued

Aisha is the Founder and CEO of Showtime Century Movies Ltd. She specialises in creating opportunities for people in the fields of acting, film production and marketing. Here is her story on how Antonio Smith Jr changed her life.

My name is Aisha Namawejje a.k.a Tetubatya. Am 27 years old from Africa, Uganda. I was born in a family of 7 girls and 2 boys of which am the 7th in one of the slums of Kampala. I grew up with my mother in extreme poverty. We always did not have a home to stay for we were always vacated due to lack of rent. We did not always have food for breakfast, lunch and supper. My mother was a mere vegetable hawker who could hardly afford all our needs. To survive, we did domestic work for our neighbours in return for food and other small needs.

I was so intelligent at school and this earned me a lot of privileges including studying for free. This is how I managed to complete my high school. Since I could not afford going to university, I enrolled for a small course that earned me a certificate in film making. Upon completion, I did not act with this achievement since I didn't have money for starting. I always thought starting a business only needed money and plenty of money!

I left the province I was living in and moved to town to look for money. However, everything I tried failed. I got tired of trying again and again. I lost a place of shelter and turned out homeless. I became so angry with myself and angry with the world, I became so resentful to life and lost hope. I devalued my life and even became depressed to the point that I attempted suicide!, Each day I woke up, I would curse myself. I thought that I was unlucky and all forms of negativity took shelter in me!

One day earlier this year, I was scrolling through my newsfeed on Facebook. I landed on a Facebook post that said, "Why do they have it all and you don't have anything?" It was something like that but what I clearly remember it was from Antonio Smith Jr. I did not know him by then, he wasn't my friend but a mutual friend. It was like he was God sent. Upon reading it, I did not rest my mind the whole day. It is as if he was referring to me. I mean I had lost everything. Who else could he have meant other than me?

I became so curious about the post as I was eager and desperate to have it all. The main problem was how? I rushed straight to my messenger and sent a message to Antonio. I wrote, "Hey Antonio how did you do it? I wanna have it all too". He never answered to me straight away. This made me more curious and I thought to myself, 'this man is a millionaire, how comes he still values people with nothing?' I can never forget how he responded. His reply changed my attitude up to now. I look up to it and in fact, I read it every day. He said, "I worked very hard. I read a lot. I study and work on my craft every day. I create massive goals and go after them. I USE THE LAW OF ATTRACTION".

Before meeting Antonio, I did not do any of the above apart from overworking! I did not believe it works. At this point, what came into my mind was that since Antonio is in the United States of America, maybe he was lucky and that is why he succeeded. I texted him again and provokingly asked him, "Hey man, what if am not lucky like you were, how can I succeed? Must I follow those same tricks you used". This was because I did not believe him by then! Antonio disclosed something to me that made me cry. He replied, 'I wasn't lucky. I grew up in a dumpster as a protection'.

At this point, I realised how life was hard for him and all the kind of suffering he might have encountered. This was the same thing I was going through. Later on, I re-read his conversation and saw something again. He talked about using the law of attraction in his journey. I asked him about it too. He did not hesitate to share it with me. I can say, he is such a golden hearted creature: so kind, loving and desperate to see everyone succeed even at no pay! God bless Antonio T Smith Jr.

Antonio sent me the link to the free courses about the 42 laws of attraction and I confess this is what changed me completely. I discovered THE SECRET. I realised one can think and grow rich. I have learnt and still learning a lot of things from him.

I call him my rescuer! I went back and re started pursuing my career as an actress and script writer. Right now I have been featured in 3 movies in just 3 months. I have got a big project to write a script for one producer and make a movie for him next month through my new company. Guess what, my life is now moving on and so meaningful to me now courtesy of Antonio. He taught me:

- ✓ how to be confident
- ✓ how to attract success
- ✓ how to accept and not resist
- ✓ how to never quit
- ✓ how to influence people
- ✓ how to know deception.

I learn from him every day and follow him. I continue to fly in the clouds because of Antonio Smith. I will forever be grateful to him. He challenged and changed my life from the grave yard of negativity. Thank you Antonio T. Smith Jr.

Retired
Grace Sandles

My Money was Funny, but it Was No Laughing Matter

140

Retired

Grace Sandles is the Director of Sales with the ATS Jr. Companies, as well as the CFO of the D. Marie Group. Here is her story of how Antonio Smith changed her life.

I met Antonio through a religious organization. Both of our churches belonged to the same organization, and that is where I met him for the first time. In meeting him, I learned that he had been retired since the age of 29. When I met found that out, he was 33. Finding this out, I told myself, "If Antonio's been retired from a job for 4 years, he knows something about money." Therefore, after talking with him and getting to know him more, I asked him to help me with my finances. I was seeing more month at the end of the money, and I didn't want to live like that anymore.

He agreed to meet with me and told me he wanted to take a look at my income and expenses. We met at a Starbucks, sat down, and I had everything he asked for prepared. After looking over everything, the first thing Antonio told me was, "You need to pay yourself first." He also told me that I had unnecessary expenses and to get rid of them. I fought him on both things, especially the "pay yourself first" part. I could not understand why I needed to do that, because in my mind, if I paid myself first, I would not have enough money to pay all of my expenses. Then with the unnecessary expenses, I just felt like I needed all of those things. When Antonio got done explaining everything to me, I politely thanked him for helping me, but I couldn't see how I could do all of the things he suggested and still have enough to pay for everything.

Since I did not take Antonio's advice, more month at the end of the money went on for 2 more years. Finally, when I got tired of the way things were, I asked Antonio to sit down with me again. I told him, "I'm ready this time for real." Thankfully, he sat down with me again at Starbucks and told me the same thing he said the first time we spoke: I needed to pay myself first. Then he said something that caused a shift in my mind. He said, "How dare you pay Capital One before you pay Grace." Then it began to make sense. I finally listened. When I got rid of the unnecessary expenses and began to pay myself first, I noticed I still had enough money to pay the remainder of my bills. Since that time (which has been about 2 years now), I have been paying myself first ever since. Later on after my second sit-down with Antonio, I learned that he told his best friend and business partner, Tempestt, that I would be working with them, and that's just what happened.

Early retirement

I began teaching middle school math at the beginning of the 2006-2007 school year. I found out that I was pretty good at it, and I liked it. As the years went by, for some reason, I started to not like teaching as much as I did when I first began. After my fifth year of teaching I told my mother, who had been a teacher for over 25 years, that I did not want to teach anymore. She would tell me that I just needed a break, and I would be fine and ready to go back after summer vacation. At the time, she was right.

However, after every school year was over, the feeling of not wanting to teach anymore grew stronger. I had been working with Antonio and Tempestt on the side since my ninth year of teaching. By the end of year number ten of teaching, I was ready to give it all up: no ifs, ands, or buts about it! It was all I ever talked about and Antonio heard me. Then one day, he said to me, "I'm gonna help you retire, but you've got to trust me." I figured if he could help me get out of the financial struggle I was in, he might be able to help me retire. I agreed to trust him.

I had gone into my eleventh year of teaching with the thought of, "This is my last year." Teaching can be very stressful but Antonio had given me advice to not allow anything to stress me out; students, parents, coworkers, administrators, grading papers, lesson plans, nothing. At first, I was not taking his advice but when it finally hit me that this was it, nothing bothered me anymore. I began to enjoy my last year of teaching. I informed my principal and a few of my co-workers that I would not be returning and would actually be retiring. Of course, they would miss me and I would miss them. My principal tried to talk me out of it several times but I told her that it was time, and there was something else that was out there in the world for me to do. She understood. Some of my coworkers were happy for me and told me to go out, do what's best for me, and live my dreams. May 31, 2018 was my last day of teaching, at the age of 37. I now work full time with Antonio, Tempestt, and several other great business partners on my goals and dreams.

Among other things

Along with my finances and retirement, Antonio has also helped me overcome my anger and low self-esteem. Every time either one reared its ugly head, Antonio never shunned me. He always remembered who I was and helped me through whatever I was going through at the time. Most people wouldn't have stuck with me but he was one of the very few who did. When I got angry or was showing my low self-esteem, Antonio would quickly hold me accountable for it (he doesn't sugarcoat anything). Then he would give me advice on how to turn my situation around.

Antonio has a big heart for people. He loves helping people reach their goals and dreams. I want to tell you that when he makes the decision to help you, make sure you are prepared for it, because he is intense! He gives 100% of himself to get you to where you said you desired to be. That, in turn, makes you want to give your all. When he sets his mind to getting things done, he becomes laser focused, and nothing or no one deters him from doing so. Thank you Antonio T. Smith Jr. for helping me with my finances, helping me retire from teaching, helping me overcome anger and low self-esteem, and believing in me, even when I didn't believe in myself. You have helped me in ways I never would have imagined, and for that, I am forever grateful to you and appreciate you.

Soared
Renee South Hendricks

Real Estate Brokerage Owner, Mortgage Broker and Credit Expert

Family Change Factor

Born in Springfield, MA of Caribbean decent, with dual citizenship in the US and UK, Renee is an active Real Estate Brokerage Owner, Mortgage Broker, Financial Literacy and Credit Expert. For over 25 years, her passion her mission has been to equip and empower people become financially fit by educating them on the power of credit and financial literacy. Here is her story on how Antonio Smith changed her life.

In the early 90's when in attendance at a Tony Robbins Personal Growth and Empowerment Seminar, I was introduced and challenged to commit my life to **CANI,** which stands for **Constant and Never-Ending Improvement.** Loving this concept, I also ended up working behind the scenes over the years to help Tony with CANI at his UPW events. I have committed to this as well as introduced it to my children. After all, as Warren Buffet says, "the greatest investment that one can make is in themselves". This is part of what led me to the place where I would meet Antonio, in pursuit of personal CANI.

Our first interaction…

Nothing happens by chance… especially when you believe in Divine Connections and live life with gratitude and expectancy! Fast forward to March 2018, I registered my family (including my 2 teenagers) to attend the Les Brown Unlimited Seminar (LBU) the following month, which was going to be held locally here in Florida.

My favorite book says that it's better to give. Knowing that presenters fly in from all over the nation and in that spirit of gratitude for Les and my children's first Live Les Brown interaction, I reached out to all of the leaders and presenters that were featured on the event flyer. This is the Facebook message that I sent to Antonio:

> Good afternoon Antonio, My name is Renee South Hendricks. I am going to be attending Power Voice in Deerfield Beach with my family. I am looking forward to meeting you, learning from you and sharing what God has for you, through me and vice versa. If there is any way that I can be of assistance, prior to or during the event, please, don't hesitate to contact me directly on my cell (954)818-1815. Have a wonderfully blessed day! Thanks & Blessings, Renee

He responded with gratitude and stated, nothing at this time, but if he thought of anything he would honor my request. I didn't think anything else about it.

How we met....

April 2018, Day 2 of LBU, I entered into a breakout session and sat down in the second row waiting for the rest of the attendees to enter for the session to begin. The speaker was at the front of the room. He had a commanding presence about him and was very charismatic as he started speaking and letting us know that the topic in the program is not what he is going to talk about. Instead, he is going to make it an open Q&A and every question that is asked, he is going to answer it in such a way that would yield a 6 figure value in implementation. In addition, during the course of his session, he is going to be giving something away. He proceeded to open the floor for Q&A.

I asked the first question, "As Matthew 7:7 states, 'Ask and it will be given to you; seek and you will find; knock and the door will be opened to you.' So, may I have whatever it is that you were planning on giving away during the session?" Somewhat taken aback, he immediately sent me to the back of the room to his Business Partner, Tempestt Smith, and gave me that and so much more. This was the beginning of the many blessings that were to follow.

Mind you, after the fact, I found out that he was one of the people that I had reached out to on Facebook. That night, I researched him and I found out that he was not only a presenter, he was a homeschooling father, a Pastor, as well as he had a true heart for helping people. He lives his life from a position of abundance. Do you remember that I said, "I believe in Divine Connections"? I had already reached out to him, and neither one of us even realized at the time who the other was. Then, I posed a question, wrapped in a scripture to a Pastor… DIVINE!

Life after meeting Antonio…

Day 3 of LBU, I witnessed an interaction with Antonio and a fellow attendee that was having MAJOR ISSUES with something event related. It is at this point that I realized that not only was he a Presenter for the event, but an Event Organizer and Advisor to Les Brown working behind the scenes closely with Serena Brown, CEO to run the entire event. The way in which he dealt with the issues for this young lady, and then went above and beyond to resolve it for her, was so very moving. Anyone in his position would have to handle it, but it was the MANNER in which he took it to HEART. It wasn't just me, but everyone that was present in that room at that moment FELT IT.

During a post event casual dinner with Antonio and several other attendees, I introduced him to my family that was in attendance with me. The dinner table conversations were friendly, light, probing and intriguing all at the same time. We learned a bit more about him, his Counter Intelligence service in the US military as well as he shared with us some of how he thinks and why. I remember thinking, "this man is philosophically profound and multidimensional". He touched us all at the way he related to my 18 year old son. Most don't connect with him, especially not quickly. Predominantly because of his high level of thinking, young people his age, especially, can seldom relate. Albert Einstein wrote, "Everybody is a genius. But if you judge a fish by its ability to climb a tree, it will live its whole life believing that it is stupid." My son thoroughly enjoyed connecting with someone in his own realm as they spoke about growth, school, graduation, college, politics, Quantum Physics and global thinking. He spoke with my 16 year old daughter about her writing, Sociology, future aspirations, Pre-law & Cambridge University programs that she's enrolled in and what she enjoyed most from LBU. And then, he really went deep! I mean, people don't do this level of deep with people they just met. He sent the children away from the table for a bit, and had me introspectively analyze how and why I parent the way I do, what was working and how to effectively parent and guide truly gifted children as they were approaching major milestones and decisions in life. His perspective to help me with parenting, in front of everyone at the table… It stripped me, guided and built me back up with a new awareness, and then he challenged me moving forward. I have to say, none of us left that table the same! We exchanged contact information, took a group photo, and bid farewell.

We were in the car driving home and as we all spoke and wondered about "What just happened?", this man, Antonio T. Smith, Jr. , little did we know at that moment, had just become an unofficial member of our family, to say the least.

Life impact of Antonio...

I joined Antonio's ATS Business University (ATS) which he also opened up to my entire family. We have plugged in to the REAL WEALTH OF INFORMATION and RESOURCES that he has available. They treat all of their enrollees with dignity, respect and have found a way to make sure that we always receive value and feel valued. With all of the live, interactive Zoom meetings, it's become more of a community/family as we grow, assist and celebrate each other.

I have to say that my favorite part of ATS has been this extremely intense, 4 month, weekly, mind expanding Book Club where we delved into Napoleon Hill's "Think and Grow Rich". I have read this book several times over the years. Yet, this level of abstraction has opened it up on a whole new level. When Antonio explains his perspectives on the subjects, it is usually explained and viewed from multiple points of view: Scientific (Physics), Theological (Christian, Islamic, etc), Philosophical, Geological, Allegorical, Subjectively, Objectively including multiple laws, like the Law of Attraction (Manifestation & Vibrating with the Universe).

Understanding concepts of: Burning your Ships Faith, It takes ZERO Faith to Win...It takes 100 Billionth Percent Faith to Decide to Win and Zero Faith to Quit...It Takes 100 Billionth Percent Faith to Keep Going, Auto Suggestion, Imagination,

Decisions from Intellect and Awareness, Persistence, Enthusiasm, Subconscious Mind, Your Brain and Your Sixth Sense will never be the same again.

Beyond business

Remember, I said that I believe in Divine Connections. Antonio has become a real mentor to my son, who has found a kindred spirit in him. They speak on the phone, share special milestones as he encourages him to pursue his dreams. There are days when I talk to him after he comes home from school (now a College Freshman) and he tells me of the steps he has made toward his dreams and how Antonio will be so proud of him.

My own awareness has leveled up in a way that can only happen when you **Surround Yourself with Greatness** and have **Eagle Conversations** that will help you to **Soar**! My Faith allows me to attract and keep Quality People in my life. Antonio is not only a Business Consultant, caring and attentive Mentor to my children and Family Confidante, but I am proud to call him my friend.

Soldier Up
Scott Fortune IV

**President of Fortune International
Seminars LLC**

www.scottdfortune.com

HS
FORTUNE
INTERNATIONAL SEMINARS
GO ON, GO AFTER IT, GO GET IT!

Soldier Up

I was born in Columbus, Ohio to my parents Scott D Fortune Sr. and Gwendolyn Hayes-Lord. Not long after birth we would move a few miles south to a small country town Wilmington, Ohio. My father had experience and background in cosmetology, youth juvenile detention officer, and as a machinist at a local factory that built machines and robotics for other factories.

We lived a normal family life as a family and experienced the American dream, when after moving from house to house, we moved to a brand new home in a middle class neighborhood in the south side of town. We would not live here a great deal of time and following the separation and divorce of my parents and the loss of my father's good paying job, we would ultimately loose the house to foreclosure.

My father was left homeless and forced to find a way to raise three kids on his own, my sister, brother and I. In the face of adversity and the challenges of life, it would be some of my closest family members that would tell my dad to give up and place my sister, brother and I in a foster home. Regardless of the struggle and how bad things would become, it was my father who stood strong in the midst of the storm and said "with Gods help I will raise my three children".

We would later be forced to live in our car in the

driveway of my grandmother's home and during the school season forced to wake up early in the car and go inside to take a bath in one shared tub of water or from the sink. The car parked in the driveway was also where our bus stop was located so every morning was a race against time to save ourselves the embarrassment of being seen living in the car. Our struggle would continue for many years as my father would work odd jobs to keep food in our stomachs and clothes on our backs.

We had to depend on the government for welfare assistance and would often find ourselves out in trash cans and ditches looking for aluminum cans and in the winter shoveling snow in the upscale neighborhoods of our community to make extra money to cover the basic necessities of life. We moved into a brand new apartment complex that was designed for low income families which was our version of the projects and backed by our local church. Things would slowly turn around when my dad, years later, crossed the picket lines and began working in a factory that made automotive parts.

Regardless of how difficult our situation was, it was my father who would continue to encourage my sister, brother, and I to pursue a path in life that would set each of us up for success. Based on the adversity and challenges of our past, my father challenged each one of us to leave town upon graduation from school and get in a position to accept the better opportunities in life. Based on these known and some untold struggles this would launch each of us to leave our small town after we graduated from high school. After graduating school in June of 1989; I would enlist and leave for the United States Army where I still serve to this very day reaching the rank of Master Sergeant and a retirement in December 2019.

I had the honor and privilege of meeting Antonio T Smith Jr. in the summer of 2017, where each of us were enrolled in The Les Brown Maximum Achievement Team where we were being directly mentored and trained by the top speaker in the industry Les Brown. Antonio and I sat at the same table and it was here where it was clear why his energy and stature attracted my attention to him.

While sitting at the table with Antonio, I heard first hand his compelling story and learned that he too served our great country in the United States Army. Antonio not only stood out from the other speakers in our large class but his very presence demanded the attention of many others. Right away, you could see that Antonio lived a purpose driven life and based on his story he has deeply rooted himself in a foundation where he used his life experience to demand better for himself and others.

One would think that based on his story and the circumstance of life, Antonio would seek ways to find ways to only benefit himself but that could not be further from the truth. Since meeting Antonio, I have seen firsthand how he uses his time and energy to coach and mentor, training others to demand more for themselves and their families.

Antonio has big clients who pay a lot of money to be personally coached, mentored and trained but what really speaks to my heart is how he took extra care and attention when I would call him on the phone. Antonio would not push me off to his staff but would directly handle my calls and pour out his heart and knowledge to me to get me to the next level.

Antonio is a giver and not only a giver but he gives over and above of himself and what he has to see to it that regardless of where you are in life that you are able to step up to the next level I would often feel guilty at times talking to Antonio because more often than not the talks were actually coaching sessions that I did not pay a dime for.

The talks would leave me desiring more of what he had to offer and I would find myself, regardless of where I was or traveling, tapping into his weekly *Let's talk Tuesday* calls being a sponge and soaking up all of his teachings.

Antonio believes in the Law of Attraction and thinking your way to success and I am proud to say that based on the teachings of our mentor Mr. Les Brown and all that I have learned from Antonio T Smith Jr., it was these teaching that gave me the confidence to step outside of my own comfort zones and to take that leap out of the nest and grow my wings on the way down.

With that said it was Antonio that also encouraged me get out in the arena of life and begin sharing my story on my own speaking tour around the country. I have often been told to "leap out of the nest and grow your wings on the way down". I have witnessed with my own eyes the following that Antonio has and the incredible staff he has working selflessly at his ATS Business University to get others to better.

Antonio puts himself in positions to win and circles himself with others who are winners and each of them are doing all they can do to leave inheritance keys for others to pick up and open doors for themselves. These keys that will be here forever long after he is gone and living the ultimate life we all seek to live, no ton earth but in heaven. Antonio validates that when we are faced with adversity and the challenges of life, we have two options to lie there and give up, or bounce back to accomplish your mission, goals, and dreams in life. It's a mindset and when we Soldier Up we get in life all that we are fighting for.

Thank you Antonio T. Smith Jr for being that beacon of light and hope for others.

Success
Marjorie Merrill

Ordained Minister, Speaker, Fashion Stylist and Author

www.MarjorieMerrillUnlimited.com

Kjærlighet og Fred • Peace • Vrede • Paz • Fred • Pace • Paix • Eine friedvolle Weihnachtszeit

Success

Marjorie Merrill is a published author, spiritual and life coach, healer, poet, speaker, stylist and ordained minister. Starting with her own, she has helped many people transform their lives with her soul stirring and mind growing messages of hope, empowerment and transformation for over 30 years. She gives people tools, tips and methods on how to tap into their true identity and innate divinity. Here is her story.

I am a well-seasoned in time, well-oiled by love and life's challenges, spiritually clothed in a magnificent edaphus of divine, unlimited, creative, spiritual energy, and operating as a divine being of this ever expansive unlimited universe in my own universal way! Historically tortured by an overtly abusive and torturous past, I could not tap into my divinity for the genius of my Divine Creator within and all around me had literally eluded me. I could get a few steps closer to success and unconsciously sabotage it! God had blessed me with gifts and talents to change the world but my broken inner child was for so long too broken to succeed!

I prayed and prayed, and prayed. I practiced healing the unconscious blockages. I had been told I was stupid as a child, unlovable, unlikeable, careless, and incapable of handling money. Along with the mental, physical and verbal abuses, I was physically abused not just by my mother but also by our racist society!

Initially, my mother tried to abort me! By the time I was 22, I had attempted suicide 3 times! This happened at the ages 3, 7 and 10. I had almost drowned due to parental negligence three times from ages 7 to 10. They were immature teenagers, my mother and my father: one a narcissist and other a workaholic…me, as shared above.

At the age of 16 soon to be 17, while carrying my firstborn and in protection of him, not even fathoming that my unborn son could be hurt; very sadly he was kicked to death while still in my womb, and died from a blow to the head from a crazed stranger, the very next day! A lots more to that story in my next book…tears fall, even now! I was most always unconsciously feeling rejected, neglected, abandoned, unloved, unlikeable, inadequate, and unlovable! It was that horrific paradigm that would shape most of my life's experiences.

My mother even told me that if I had not been acting more like a child as oppose to far beyond my years, maybe someone would like me! I did not know that these abuses created a paradigm that would affect my ability to love myself and create a life of self-sufficiency for most of my life. Despite the brilliance of the Divine being my true nature, I would not allow myself to move beyond the childhood paradigm of abuse as I did not know how! By the time I was 15, my boyfriend and future father of my child shot me in my foot with a 32~caliber pistol.

Antonio T. Smith Jr. Changed Our Lives

Between ages 17 and 24, was raped 4 different times: once at gunpoint and once at the point of strangulation. I thought he was going to kill me while my babies were downstairs in my ultimately repossessed car. It is the same man who had raped me at gunpoint who strangled me and stole the money I had borrowed from a loan company to move to a new home. Due to eviction and homelessness, my children and I ended up living at my Mother's and step-father's sharing the home with their children. My children and I were Cinderella, basically! The greatest news is that I did a lot of self-work; praying, reading, meditating, practicing, healing and cleaning this mess. In this journey, I was helped by a young genus, successful, generous, spiritually grounded successful, multi-millionaire businessman and millionaire maker Mr. Antonio T. Smith Jr. who came into my life and began to rock my world with unlimited possibilities!!!

Antonio is my adopted heart son! He embodies the spirit of my son who was killed! He has the heart and soul of an angel and the brilliant mind of a God. He is changing so many people every day helping us to not only see the path but by walking the path with us. He is a heart-centered entrepreneur. His methods have helped me and others who did not believe in ourselves or who did not believe that it was possible to reach a level of success, happiness, and fulfillment even in the midst of our messes!

The ATS Business University, Private Mastermind

Group, and People Who Plant Better is changing my life tremendously. It is giving me a family of likeminded individuals who desire to see me succeed as much as I desire to see myself succeed and vice-versa. The awesome communities that he and his wife Tempestt, my heart daughter, have created speaks volumes as to why they and their companies are so very successful. My life will be forever indebted to Antonio and Tempestt Smith: two of the most awesome, loving and giving people I know. They are game changers in the world of business. Prayerfully, every other entrepreneur will follow their lead and success for all will be a dream come true of theirs and mine!

I love you, my Son, Antonio T. Smith Jr! I know that you will keep rising to the top and remain while everyone you can, you will take them with you…and so will we, your protégés in business!

Unchurched
Tonia R Griffin

Founder of Khambrel Foundation
www.khambrelfoundation.org

Unchurched

Tonia is the CEO of Khambrel Foundation which provides reading programs and incentives to encourage building our children's dreams now. Her foundation partners with Day Cares, Libraries, Elementary Schools and Community organizations working with children ages 1-5 building dreams one book at a time. Khambrel Foundation also connects youth ages 6-17 and their families with hands on educational and financial literacy day camps, conferences, community outreach and small group activities designed to strengthen goals and dreams. It supports single-parent families and community organizations in need of food, clothes and household product donations. Here is her story on how Antonio Smith Jr changed her life.

As former Senior Director of Pastoral Care and Executive Director of Ministries for Church for the Unchurched and Project Manager, Marketing Director, Director of Marketing and Strategic Planning for Without An Umbrella Ministries, I remember the first time I saw Rev Antonio Smith hit my Facebook newsfeed. He was looking for kingdom minded people and I loved kingdom building. I messaged Antonio my area of interest and immediately received a job description to which I replied I would be joining him within 30 days.

Following a one-on-one meeting outlining the vision and mission of Church for the Unchurched, I received an email with a link instructing me to take an assessment designed to identify my strengths and weakness. At first, I thought it was an assessment to ensure I do not let my Baptist mentality keep me from reaching the unchurched. It assessed me based on my answers to certain beliefs and situations. I was very pleased with the results as they were spot on but more importantly we were afforded a leadership class to teach us who we were and what type of heart was needed to reach others globally.

I grew up a hardcore Baptist and there were certain things that were not allowed in church. Here I was joining Church for the Unchurched where everyone belongs but there was nothing traditional about this Baptist Church. The first visit I was a nervous wreck and my palms were sweating profusely. I was now a part of an openly inclusive church that found a way to connect the unchurched bringing them closer to Christ. The services were 1 hour and 15 minutes and available in-person, online or via the phone. It was amazing nothing traditional about this church and the leadership Antonio was bringing to the Galveston County, Texas area. He never wanted to remain comfortable on any level always thinking of ways to lead the unchurched yet providing leadership classes that included the opportunity for many to build financial intelligence and their own economy. As leaders, we were being equipped to led ministries, build businesses, author books and train those who desired to learn beyond the bible.

As a Pastor, Antonio maximized his theological education to make sure the unchurched was able to understand each message that was being shared to help create a bond of understanding between the word as it is written in the Bible and the world today. He was able to break the tradition of old and still fulfill his commandments to teach all nations.

Antonio also had a connection to the people from his days of being homeless as a child and growing up in the streets. Without An Umbrella Ministries provided an opportunity to give back to the community hosting the annual We Care Events, speaking at homeless shelters, donating to the veteran community and mentoring to the youth in the juvenile system. Antonio has developed a strong desire to not leave anyone behind always serving as an ear on the other end of the phone providing the help necessary to keep pushing forward.

Fast forward September 2014, we were presented with the Integrity Leadership Course targeting the heart of a leader. It was like none I had ever seen: 10 books in 10 months. Then every we had to turn in a reflective paper the 1st Wednesday of every month. For those of us wanting to be leaders, it was like we were in a free school and never been exposed to small groups discussions. This course has helped stir up hidden dreams in many of those who took the first step. If you were to take a poll "Where Are They Now?", you would find many Life Coaches, Authors, CEOs, Entrepreneurs, Business Owners and Non-Profit Organizations being launched because of the seeds being planted better.

I myself started a Non-Profit Organization in honor of my mother and granddaughter helping others and serving others. It is not often that you get to disclose those who were with you in the gym and the opportunity to thank them publicly. The key is to always remain true to your vision, mission and purpose which is easy to follow even when the method is constantly changing. I was still a little miss guided and eager to achieve all of my goals and accomplishments now. I needed help with all of my sticky notes, memos and handwritten napkins organizing them into viable goals and things to accomplish now.

Antonio scheduled a consultation to help develop a business plan for Khambrel Foundation going beyond sending links to important resources to read on or groups to become a part of. I can never thank him enough for the seeds he leaves behind to help others become better. I've been part of the movement as Antonio moved from an apartment, to a building, to a center and to a church.

With his B.A., M.A.T.S. and the many accolades, Antonio is destined to receive I do believe Antonio T. Smith, Jr. Companies, Brick-by-Brick Top Ranked Business Podcast and Plant Better University is only the beginning for Antonio. If you simply sit back and return to where we started, you will find there is a supreme destiny on your life, where you are taught to become the highest expression of your life. Stay grounded and focused and never let God's favor cause you to step outside of yourself.

It is an honor to receive such valuable input, you helped bring out the best in me. All of those leadership books that I fought so hard not to read, they impact my decision to include reading and financial literacy programs for youth helping to impact their goals, dreams and leadership abilities. I was in attendance the day Antonio T. Smith, Jr. declared he was going to Plant Better and Build Economies. I saw no limits in his eyes and his exact words were "I Am Here To Dominate".

University
Dr Patrick Businge

Author, Celebrity Researcher and Founder of Greatness University

www.greatness-university.com

University

In Summer 2017, my wife and I were hungry to achieve our dream of becoming international speakers and coaches. Our deep hunger put us on a journey from London in England to Fort Lauderdale in Florida. We were going to start a life changing mentorship programme with Les Brown: the world's greatest motivational speaker.

When we reached the Doubletree by Hilton Hotel in Deerfield Beach, Fort Lauderdale, the venue where the Certification was to take place, we discovered that we just had seeing missed Les Brown during the meet and greet session. The next day, Les Brown came to the stage. As I listened to Les Brown speak, at one point he said, 'we are sold everything except one product: greatness'. He went on to say, 'You have something special, you have greatness within you'. He then added, 'The graveyard is the richest place on earth, because it is here that you will find all the hopes and dreams that were never fulfilled, the books that were never written, the songs that were never sung, the inventions that were never shared, the cures that were never discovered, all because someone was too afraid to take that first step, keep with the problem, or determined to carry out their dream'.

As I listened to Les Brown speaking, his message quickly travelled from my head and dwelt in my heart. This triggered an inner conversation with myself. Here is how it went: 'Many people are born and live without knowing that they have a great treasure in them: greatness. They end up dying without ever living to their full potential because they are not aware of their greatness. What if I made a business that focused on greatness? This will surely help them discover their greatness and live a great life'. This conversation effected a change in me that was beyond my wildest dreams.

My intention of coming to the Certification in Florida was not to start a business but to learn how to become a better speaker and coach. During the certification, each person was called to introduce himself or herself. Among us was Antonio T. Smith Jr who, when called to introduce himself, brought his whole team to the stage. During this time, he talked about having an online university. As I took the flight back to the United Kingdom, I pondered on how I was to put into practice my idea of creating products around greatness. Upon my return to England, I created Greatness University that I wished to look like Antonio's Plant Better University.

As I did not have the platform, I called Antonio Smith who freely gave me ideas on how to go about having an online university. Since then, Antonio has been my consultant on various business ideas and research projects without whom some would have not been realised. He wrote a Foreword for my book '7 Steps to Greatness' for free: a Foreword that someone else had asked me to pay him $15,000.

Today, Greatness University prides itself as the world's first institution dedicated to researching and monetising greatness. At Greatness University, we believe that greatness leaves clues. We are therefore committed to helping people tap into their greatness faster and easily than they can ever imagine. We do this by researching greatness in individuals, organizations, businesses, and other spheres of life. We help people create their personal economies by monetising their greatness. We guide people on the best ways to create a lasting legacy. Remember, legacy is not what you give to the people you love but what you leave in them.

Indeed, Antonio Smith's generosity has allowed me to help people discover, develop, and deliver their greatness. May his greatness continue to shine and illuminate the path for millions of people who are looking for a way to win in life.

Afterword
Tempestt S. Smith

CEO of ATS Jr. Companies

Afterword

As I have read through the words on the previous pages, I couldn't help but to smile. As someone who actually knows Antonio T. Smith Jr. pretty well, I am not surprised by anything that I have read. Nothing unlike his character is mentioned which only confirms that the same Antonio I know, is the same Antonio the world gets to see every single day. If I could sum up this book and everyone's input on Antonio into one word, it would be: dominate.

Antonio is a listener. He is a giver. He is a doer. He is a leader amongst leaders that allows his followers to lead. Many spoke on how well-heard they feel whenever they talk to him. He has prided himself on mastering how to actively listen. Many spoke on how much time, effort, energy and resources he freely gives that others would charge for. Sometimes he gives so much to the extent that he does not have time to give to himself. He constantly and consistently digs deep and gives everyone, everything within him, even if it appears that they do not deserve it. He leads. Not many know this, but being remember as an excellent leader is how he wants to leave this earth. After reading through everyone's stories, I hope he sees that he doesn't have to wait until death to be honored and celebrated as a leader.

When I first met Antonio, he would tell people, "I am the leader you are looking for". While others may say the same, his words have proven to be true, time and time again. That's the thing about true leaders, they come when you least expect it. They lead by demonstrating. They lead by giving. They lead by dominating.

Everything that everyone has said, all comes back to Antonio's determination to dominate and to even force others to wake up and to do the same in their own lives. At times, it is intimidating to learn from him, to watch him and to create with him, but when I think of stopping, when I think of giving up, I consider that a 6-year-old child, who was left abandoned by his parents and his entire family, survived the "unsurviveable." When I consider that that same 6-year-old grew up and served his country, served his community, serves those around him and serves everyone he comes in contact with, I understand why it is necessary to dominate.

We are given one shot at this life. Just one and the more we wake up and make it through the day safely, the more we take that same life for granted. But not Antonio. When he says he ends his day empty, he literally means he ends the day on empty. Whether it is helping to build ministries, coaching people how to jump-start their lives, consult individuals who have a dream but no idea how to put his or her dreams into motion, being an amazing father who somehow runs multiple companies, helps thousands and manages to homeschool his kids who are excited and ready to learn about business, science, math, economics and any and everything in between, Antonio dominates.

I hope that as you are closing this book, you learn that time is of the essence and you begin to not only show up for your life, but dominate it like only you can.

As Antonio T. Smith Jr. says, you can plant better. You can dominate.

Tempestt S. Smith

About the Author

Born in in Uganda, Dr Patrick Businge did not let his circumstances characterised by war and abject poverty become his standard. Following his dreams while believing that no condition was permanent, he took steps to raise above his circumstances and made greatness his benchmark.

Dr Patrick Businge has gone on to become the Founder of Greatness University: the world's first institution dedicated to discovering, unlocking, and monetising greatness in individuals and businesses. His main goal is to help you tap into your greatness faster than you can ever imagine. He has helped celebrities, business people, and churches document their greatness. His past research projects include:

- **Les Brown Changed Our Lives**: 77 Stories to Inspire You to Live Your Dreams
- **Jesus Changed Our Lives**: Stories From The Heart To Enrich Your Faith
- **Antonio T Smith Jr Changed Our Lives**: Stories To Inspire You To Plant Better
- **The City of Refuge Changed Our Lives**: Stories to Inspire You to Take Refuge in God.

Dr Patrick Businge is a bestselling author and has written and co-authored various books including:

- 7 Steps to Greatness: The **Masterplan** to Take Your Life, Studies, Career and Business to the Next Level

- 7 Steps to Greatness: The **Workbook** to Take Your Life, Studies, Career and Business to the Next Level
- 7 Steps to Greatness: The **Journal** to Take Your Life, Studies, Career and Business to the Next Level
- The Road to Your Best Self: Discover Your Miracle Power, Uncommon Nature and the Greatness in You
- 7 Steps to Become A Bestselling Author: Discover, Develop and Deliver the Book in You.

Having grown up in Uganda: a country characterised by war, plagued by a shortage of hope and marred with average performance, Dr Patrick Businge's ultimate vision is to inspire one million people become instruments of peace, messengers of hope and channels of greatness. He runs transformational seminars, offers exciting talks and conducts celebrity research. It is because of his vision, insight, and contribution to humanity that he was awarded the Authentic Leadership Award.

To learn more about his programs, seminars, and commission him to write a book on how you have changed people's lives please visit **www.greatness-university.com**. If you have any personal questions email him directly at info@greatness-university.com or meet him on Facebook, LinkedIn and Instagram.

Antonio T. Smith Jr. Changed Our Lives

www.ingramcontent.com/pod-product-compliance
Lightning Source LLC
Chambersburg PA
CBHW051245050726
47594CB00001B/322